Proactivity in Economics

Between plain resourcefulness and full-blooded entrepreneurship lies a middle ground of proactivity which, as this book argues, is a concept that allows economists to make better sense of activity where an individual takes greater agency over their personal outcomes through the existing employment or additional activity.

In this way, proactivity can help economists develop greater understanding of undervalued or understudied areas such as employee self-initiative, protean career orientation, gig contracting, and prosumer activism. In theoretical terms: if economics is perceived as the investigation of the logic of human action, this book presents the case for the concept of proactivity being seen as a vital aspect of the process whereby economic agents bring about more desirable states of affairs with the use of scarce means. Through their proactiveness, individuals can combine several conventionally defined economic roles (e.g., conscious consumers and independent producers or frontline workers and quasi-entrepreneurs) and sources of income (e.g. regular wages and performance-based quasi-profits or regular wages and minority shareholder profits). In turn, this makes it possible to identify previously underappreciated sources of economic growth and furnishes additional arguments against ideas – such as economic nationalism – whose implementation is likely to stunt the productive potential of individuals.

This book will be of interest to readers in economic theory, entrepreneurship, economic development, and behavioral economics.

Jakub Bożydar Wiśniewski is Assistant Professor in the Faculty of Law, Administration, and Economics at the University of Wrocław, Wrocław, Poland; a member of the Board of Trustees of the Ludwig von Mises Institute for Economic Education, Wrocław, Poland; and a Fellow of the Mises Institute.

Routledge Focus on Economics and Finance

The fields of economics are constantly expanding and evolving. This growth presents challenges for readers trying to keep up with the latest important insights. Routledge Focus on Economics and Finance presents short books on the latest big topics, linking in with the most cutting-edge economics research.

Individually, each title in the series provides coverage of a key academic topic, whilst collectively the series forms a comprehensive collection across the whole spectrum of economics.

The Circular Economy and SMEs
Edited by Fahimeh Khatami

Financial Security and Household Life Insurance
Bridging the Gap
Joanna Dębicka and Anna Jędrzychowska

Corporate Short-Term Financing in Europe
The Role of Trade Credit and Bank Loans in Liquidity Management
Julia Koralun-Bereźnicka

Financial Resilience and the Sustainable Development Goals
Edited by Magdalena Zioło and Bruno S. Sergi

Geopolitics, China, and the Global Supply Chain
Issues and Implications
Sarah Chan

Proactivity in Economics
Between Resourcefulness and Entrepreneurship
Jakub Bożydar Wiśniewski

For more information about this series, please visit: www.routledge.com/Routledge-Focus-on-Economics-and-Finance/book-series/RFEF

Proactivity in Economics

Between Resourcefulness and Entrepreneurship

Jakub Bożydar Wiśniewski

Routledge
Taylor & Francis Group
LONDON AND NEW YORK

First published 2026
by Routledge
4 Park Square, Milton Park, Abingdon, Oxon OX14 4RN

and by Routledge
605 Third Avenue, New York, NY 10158

Routledge is an imprint of the Taylor & Francis Group, an informa business

British Library Cataloguing-in-Publication Data
A catalogue record for this book is available from the British Library

ISBN: 978-1-041-28422-2 (hbk)
ISBN: 978-1-041-28424-6 (pbk)
ISBN: 978-1-003-76455-7 (ebk)

DOI: 10.4324/9781003764557

Typeset in Times New Roman
by Apex CoVantage, LLC

Contents

Introduction

"Proactivity" is a term that has frequently come to be regarded as little more than a good-sounding buzzword, sharing the same fate as similarly overused terms such as "sustainability", "resilience", "disruption", and "inclusion". And yet, it is my belief that, perhaps in contrast to the rest of the abovementioned examples, it can, if used with analytical caution, still serve as a potent source of constructive insights capable of yielding interdisciplinary gains from trade in the realm of the social sciences.

More specifically, while so far the phenomenon of proactivity has been explored primarily in the fields of psychology and organization theory, I believe that it continues to be underutilized in economics – in particular, in pure economic theory as opposed to narrowly focused empirical case studies dealing with workplace environments or industry dynamics. If, in what is perhaps its most methodologically ambitious formulation, economics is to be conceived as the investigation of the logic of human action, proactivity can be seen as a vital, though hitherto understudied, aspect of the process whereby intentional agents substitute more desirable for less desirable states of affairs with the use of scarce means.

In a similar vein, the study of the phenomenon of entrepreneurship, long neglected in mainstream economics, has been instrumental in developing realistic theories of pricing, competition, and business cycles, bringing into focus such crucial elements of economic decision-making as uncertainty, expectations, learning, and creativity. My goal in the present work is to continue along the same lines by offering an economically grounded exposition of a concept that is broader than that of entrepreneurship, but narrower than that of self-motivation or resourcefulness, thereby hopefully hitting the golden mean between restricted disciplinary focus and wishy-washy vagueness.

It is my hope to demonstrate that just as the neglect of entrepreneurship prevented economic theorists from making good sense of phenomena such as firm formation, price arbitrage, product innovation, and asset speculation, the neglect of proactivity can prevent them from making good sense of phenomena such as employee self-initiative, protean career orientation, gig contracting, and prosumer activism. That is to say, it can prevent them from, on the

DOI: 10.4324/9781003764557-1

one hand, underappreciating the quasi-entrepreneurial potential of ordinary wage earners and, on the other hand, overstating the degree to which business organisms can be run in an egalitarian and participatory fashion.

In line with the saying that there is nothing more practical than a good theory, the above approach serves as a telling reminder that reflecting on various newly emergent phenomena can be the best starting point for expanding the theoretical edifice of the discipline used to study them. This, in turn, may result in a deepened understanding of the developments under consideration, their potential going forward, and the prerequisites for their survival. Hence, in the subsequent chapters, I shall identify what I regard as some of the most quintessential manifestations of proactivity, attempt to pin down their origins, describe their analytical ramifications, investigate the prospective benefits of their widespread dissemination, and comment on what I take to be the most pressing challenges to reaping these benefits.

The structure of the present book is as follows. In Chapter 1, I shall elaborate on the transition from what might be called the currently prevailing "managerial society" to the gradually emerging proactive society, placing special attention on distinguishing between entrepreneurship and proactivity, the former being a functionally narrow concept and the latter being its much broader and formally looser extension. Then, I shall discuss several categories of characteristics of the proactive society, including those of a structural, organizational, political, ethical, and cognitive nature.

Having thus provided a fairly comprehensive overview of the titular socioeconomic system, in Chapter 2, I shall examine the issue of how the advent of the proactive society can help advance various areas of economic theory, including considerations of scarcity, value, capital, production, monopoly, competition, welfare, distribution, employment, labor, rationality, and efficiency. In doing so, I shall attempt to bring into sharper focus, among other things, the qualitative character of scarcity, the educational character of employment, the multidimensional character of welfare, and the processual character of efficiency. I shall also try to demonstrate that such theoretical refinements can, in turn, help in making the most of the novel developments that led to their formulation.

In Chapter 3, I shall look at what appear to me to be the main economic, social, and cognitive challenges capable of stopping the transition from the managerial society to the proactive society in its tracks or even reversing it. By the same token, I shall attempt to identify the "allies" of the latter, that is, the beliefs, attitudes, expectations, and values whose widespread adoption is essential in fostering the proactive mindset together with the recognition of both its opportunities and demands. More specifically, I shall point out that cultivating the mindset in question requires, among others, resisting both the utopianism of "post-scarcity" and the misguided "realism" of anti-globalization, thereby necessitating opposition both to the allure of "technological emancipation" from labor and to the blandishments of "protection" from the vagaries of international trade.

Finally, in the concluding section, I shall try to underscore the uniqueness of the proactive society by sketching a brief historical narrative in which the titular system is compared favorably with its consecutive predecessors. There, I shall emphasize that proactivity, treated as an inherent – though often dormant – element of human action, can be justifiably regarded as the ultimate meta-factor of production, whose constructive use determines the productivity of various combinations of the remaining factors: land, labor, capital, and even entrepreneurship. In addition, I shall stress that the proactive orientation can be best promoted by concerted efforts of distinct social groups – researchers, entrepreneurs, costumers, etc. – all of whom can exhibit its unique and mutually reinforcing manifestations in their respective lines of occupation, thereby demonstrating its beneficial potential with particular visibility.

With this, let me now proceed to the first chapter, in which the nature of the proactive society, together with its manifold defining characteristics, will be discussed in greater detail.

1 The nature of the proactive society

1.1 Setting the conceptual stage

It has become a well-established contention in the specialist literature that the so-called managerial society of the previous century is increasingly giving way to the so-called entrepreneurial society (Audretsch, 2009). However, while the latter concept is almost uniformly associated with terms such as dynamism, adaptability, and personal initiative, its precise definition remains as elusive as the definition of entrepreneurship itself (Ahmad and Seymour, 2008).

As far as its most popular characterizations go, entrepreneurship is variously described as alertness to profit opportunities, introduction of innovations, and uncertainty bearing. Thus, I believe that a truly compelling definition of the concept in question should be capable of meaningfully subsuming all of the above phenomena without simultaneously making the matter denoted by it so vague as to render it analytically useless.

The characterization of entrepreneurship that appears to me to best satisfy the above requirement is the one that treats it as the exercise of the ownership function over capital structures of production under conditions of uncertainty (Foss and Klein, 2012). Both Schumpeterian innovators and Kirznerian arbitrageurs derive profits from successfully configuring and reconfiguring their own scarce resources in the face of uncertain future, which makes them both members of an analytically distinct group of market participants while still allowing for seeing their activities as functionally heterogeneous (Kirzner, 2009). Furthermore, the characterization in question allows for treating the activities of Schumpeterian and Kirznerian entrepreneurs as functionally complementary and mutually reinforcing (Holcombe, 2003), the former upsetting the existing market equilibrium by introducing qualitatively novel data and the latter restoring a new, qualitatively more advanced equilibrium by making this data sufficiently widely disseminated. In sum, this particular approach to entrepreneurship, otherwise known as the judgment-based view, coherently unifies the most influential definitions of entrepreneurial action under the aegis of a robust theory of property, capital, and the firm, thereby

DOI: 10.4324/9781003764557-2

providing a comprehensive vision of what constitutes the essence of the market process (Kirzner, 2017).

However, it should be noted here that the entrepreneurial society is typically defined as involving the extension of specifically entrepreneurial duties and responsibilities to hired managers and other non-owning employees. More specifically, its descriptions often emphasize the increasing relevance of phenomena such as intrapreneurship (De Jong and Wennekers, 2008) and effectual thinking (Sarasvathy, 2008), which do not apply exclusively to the activities of entrepreneurs understood as owners of firms and the ultimate exercisers of business judgment. Thus, one might wonder whether the judgment-based view of entrepreneurship, with its emphasis on capital ownership, truly captures the essence of the emerging entrepreneurial society.

In response, it might be argued that the entrepreneurial mindset is not an all-or-nothing phenomenon, but rather an ideal type that can be attained more or less completely, firm owners being the ones who approximate it most fully, intrapreneurs being the ones who approximate it to a lesser degree, and regular employees being the ones who are generally distant from it. It might then be argued that the entrepreneurial society is one in which the mindset in question assumes an unprecedented importance, whereby hired managers and other non-owners of corporate assets are increasingly expected to act as if they too bear ultimate responsibility for the operations of the firms they work for.

If, however, one were to insist that business judgment cannot be separated from property ownership, then striving to exercise the entrepreneurial mindset even in a non-owning capacity could be designated by another term: proactivity. Proactivity, defined as the willingness to act on one's own accord in advance of future contingencies (Grant and Ashford, 2008; Frese and Gielnik, 2014), can be reasonably regarded as the essence of entrepreneurial attitude, but it can be exhibited by owner-entrepreneurs and their employees alike. Thus, perhaps a more appropriate name for the emerging successor of the 20th century managerial society would be the "proactive society". As this particular term appears to capture the gist of modern economic dynamism and innovativeness without making the corresponding concept of entrepreneurship either too broad or too narrow, I shall henceforward use it to denote the complexity of economic and social phenomena that I wish to analyze in the subsequent sections of the present book.

In the next section of this chapter, I shall elaborate on the technological, social, and organizational reasons that necessitate the emergence of the proactive society treated as a crucial prerequisite for continued economic development and sustainable global cooperation. In Section 1.3, I shall analyze the structural principles and the general organizational shape that a robustly proactive society has to adopt if it is to retain, let alone deepen its specific cooperative advantage. In Section 1.4, I shall apply a similar analysis to the general political and administrative developments that appear to me to be particularly conducive to the actualization of the cooperative potential of widespread proactivity. In Section 1.5, I shall do the same with respect to the broadly understood ethical norms that I regard as constitutive of the essential institutional framework of the proactive society. In Section 1.6, I shall conclude with some remarks concerning the cognitive competences that encourage proactivity and allow for addressing operational challenges in a self-starting manner.

As the analytical approach adopted throughout the present work is neither occupational nor structural, but functional (Klein, 2008: 176–178), it employs primarily the insights not of psychology or sociology, but of economics. It is precisely the task of economic theory, especially that in the causal-realist tradition originating with the Mengerian strand of the marginalist revolution (Salerno, 2010), to investigate the functional essence of phenomena such as entrepreneurship, property ownership, and capital management, together with their logical preconditions and ramifications. Thus, I believe that the insights of theoretical economics are particularly well suited to providing a comprehensive conceptual overview of the emerging phenomenon of the proactive society.

Such an overview promises to be a substantial contribution to the establishment of solid economic foundations of entrepreneurship research (McCaffrey, 2018), as well as a potent illustration of the fact that economics, while being value-free, is nonetheless capable of furnishing conclusions that are normatively useful (Casey, 2012). In sum, it promises to offer cogent arguments for the claim that the entrepreneurial or proactive society, far from being a clichéd abstraction, is a concept with specific developmental origins, constitutive features, and practical implications of organizational, ethical, and political nature.

1.2 The origins of the proactive society

The reasons for the transition from the reactive society of managerial control to the proactive society of entrepreneurial initiative can be classed into at least three categories – those of technological, organizational, and broadly social character. Let us analyze these in turn.

First, consistent economic and social development is, to a significant extent, a function of implementing various kinds of innovation (Hall and Rosenberg, 2010). These, in turn, consist in large part of creating technological procedures and devices aimed at automating routine human work. These procedures and devices, while reducing the demand for repetitive and mechanical kinds of labor, also disproportionately increase the demand for the kind of labor that cannot be automated (Acemoglu and Restrepo, 2018).

The latter category consists primarily of tasks whose completion requires the use of specifically human characteristics and faculties such as introspection, imagination, empathy, creativity, and general interpersonal sensitivity. In other words, it involves responding to the beliefs, desires, judgments, and expectations of one's fellow human beings, whose internal life and external behavior do not follow any algorithmically determinable pattern. Thus, it involves moving from the realm of probabilistic risk into the realm of true uncertainty (Knight, 1985), that is, into an area where being effective requires complementing responsiveness with proactivity.

The proactivity in question need not necessarily assume the form of anticipating the future needs of customers, which is a task typically reserved for full-blooded entrepreneurs and intrapreneurial managers. In contrast, it might be mostly restricted to responding effectively to the existing needs of customers in a uniquely perceptive and creatively comprehensive manner. As interpreting customer behavior and reacting to it in the most appropriate way under the given circumstances of time and place demand a substantial degree of social imagination (Steinbauer, Rhew, Kinnamon, and Fabian, 2014), interpreting customer behavior needs to be grounded in personal initiative, thus fully qualifying as an instance of proactive conduct. In addition, it is plausible that exercising social imagination is a paradigmatic kind of activity that requires a combination of reasoned judgment (McMullen and Shepherd, 2006) and impulsive empathy (Lerner, Hunt, and Dimov, 2018), thereby embodying a broad spectrum of characteristically entrepreneurial modes of action. Finally, as consumers are increasingly identified as innovators in their own right (von Hippel, Ogawa, and de Jong, 2011), proactive tapping into their insights may be seen as a crucial task of a workforce increasingly focused on direct interaction with clients.

In sum, the foregoing remarks are perfectly consistent with the well-known observation that technological development has created far more jobs than it has destroyed (Stewart, De, and Cole, 2015), but they introduce an essential caveat to the issue at hand: as mechanical work is increasingly performed by mechanical devices, remaining productive as a human agent increasingly requires uniquely human competences, proactivity being chief among them. Thus, on the one hand, automation allows human beings to move away from jobs that are regarded as soul-crushing in their monotony and unimaginativeness, but, on the other hand, it necessitates living up to one's specifically human potential if one is to stay professionally active.

Second, consistent economic and social development goes hand in hand with capital heterogenization (Lewin and Baetjer, 2011), which, in turn, goes hand in hand with organizational complexification. Hence, as soon as a given firm surpasses a certain critical level of complexity, it becomes impossible for its owners or even its higher-level managers to supervise the activities of its nonexecutive employees and evaluate their performance on the basis of strictly technical and unambiguously interpretable criteria. Nor is it possible under such conditions to lay down meticulous task plans and assign exhaustively described, repeatable duties to specific employees. All of this follows from the fact that the greater the degree of organizational complexity, the greater the number of potential unforeseen contingencies and unique situations to deal with.

Consequently, remaining efficient under the circumstances in question necessitates promoting nonexecutive employees, and even more so those with managerial responsibilities, to the level of "proxy-entrepreneurs" (Foss, Foss, and Klein, 2007). Proxy-entrepreneurs, though they may have no personal stake in the company they work for, are nonetheless expected to exercise business judgment as part of their job requirements – that is to say, they are under an obligation to confront singular business events and make discretionary budget decisions. By the same token, their performance is assessed not on the basis of any technically specifiable indicators, but in accordance with the profit and loss yardstick provided by the ongoing market process. And as the essence of the entrepreneurial mindset (including its "proxy" form) consists in anticipating and responding to unique contingencies, assuming it requires the adoption of a proactive orientation.

In other words, proxy-entrepreneurs, just as their full-blooded counterparts, must be able to not only address already existing problems in a discretionary manner but also identify potential problems looming on the horizon, which are partially or almost entirely clouded by the veil of uncertainty. This fact provides a potent illustration of the contention that in an increasingly advanced economy, it is not just full-blown entrepreneurs that have to learn their craft by means of accumulating a substantial amount of professional experience, but their proactive employees as well. That is to say, it turns out that in a sufficiently complex business environment, even rank and file workers cannot perform well from the get-go, but, having completed relevant studies or training courses, they need to hone their skills on the basis of "convex tinkering" (Taleb, 2012), that is, decentralized experimentation, mutual learning, and slowly growing practical wisdom. Again, these are all hallmarks of proactivity.

Third, in a dynamic, globalized world characterized by rapidly changing consumer tastes, highly mobile capital, and a substantial rate of technological advance, finding a "lifetime job" is an increasingly unlikely prospect. Consequently, enjoying uninterrupted professional development under such circumstances requires pursuing not a stable and predictable career, but a "protean" one (Hall, 2004). In other words, instead of formulating precise causal plans whereby one gradually acquires the means suited to reaching a predetermined professional goal, one must be willing to continually adjust one's goals to the means obtainable in various configurations of swiftly changing market data. Thus, one needs not only to jettison "causal reasoning" in favor of "effectual reasoning" (Sarasvathy, 2008) but also to be ready to deploy such reasoning repeatedly, so as to be able to recreate one's career, sometimes almost from scratch, if the external environment changes thoroughly enough.

To put the matter somewhat differently, it might be said that adopting the "protean" approach to one's career development is akin to assuming the position of a full-blooded entrepreneur who actively organizes and manages the heterogeneous assets that comprise his individual structure of human capital.

As the value of such assets is ultimately rooted in their subjectively perceived attributes, functions, characteristics, and uses (Foss, Foss, Klein, and Klein, 2007), no coach, consultant, or mentor can replace a given individual and his personal prudential judgment when it comes to recognizing his unique talents, skills, competences, and selling propositions. If, however, one is eager to balk at the suggestion of extending the word "entrepreneur" to protean career pursuers who are still hired employees rather than business owners, then it might be convenient to call them "proactive professionals". Such a proposal is fully in line with my earlier observation that proactivity, while including numerous key qualities typically regarded as the essence of entrepreneurship, is nonetheless a significantly broader and more widely applicable concept.

An interesting question that arises in this connection has to do with how the proactive orientation fits in the spectrum between specialization and versatility. It is plausible to argue that entrepreneurs, as the ultimate custodians of their businesses, must be jacks of all trades, while their hired subordinates are expected to fulfill precisely designated, highly specialized roles (Lazear, 2004). What then are we to make of proactive career builders, who seemingly have to combine the specialized skills of highly qualified employees with the versatility of quasi-entrepreneurs in charge of their personal human capital? It would appear that the most satisfactory answer to this question is the most straightforward one: such individuals should be seen as striking the middle ground between a broad vision and a narrow focus to as great an extent as is possible. More specifically, while remaining highly qualified employees first and foremost, they simultaneously have to be constantly on the lookout for opportunities to make their specialized skillsets applicable across disciplines and professions (Bear and Skorton, 2019). While this does not require them to infuse the market with qualitatively novel data – as is the case with regard to full-blown entrepreneurs – it nonetheless does oblige them to adopt a self-starting approach when it comes to adjusting their personal "market data" to the changing configuration of external demand.

Finally, it should be emphasized that all the proactivity-inducing phenomena discussed in the preceding paragraphs – proxy-entrepreneurship, protean career building, and the growing demand for non-automatable labor – are associated not only with certain "positive" expectations but with their "negative" counterparts as well. That is to say, proactivity requires both the kind of prudence that allows for anticipating unique problems and approaching them in a self-starting manner, and the kind of caution that allows for avoiding dangers that are inherently resistant to problematization. This is because a technologically advanced, organizationally complex, and socially dynamic economy increasingly moves its participants from the domain of class probability to that of case probability (Hoppe, 2007). In other words, it moves them from the realm of repeatable events to that of singular events, where the latter are by definition uninsurable. However, uninsurability is not tantamount to unpredictability – singular events cannot be predicted on the basis of quantitative formulae or actuarial tables, but they can be at least partially predicted on the basis of sound entrepreneurial judgment (Foss and Klein, 2012). Thus, in a world growingly dominated by unique occurrences, danger avoidance is less a function of technical sophistication than it is a result of personal proactivity, especially in its prudential aspects.

In conclusion, the transition from the managerial society of hierarchical subordination to the entrepreneurial society of proactive autonomy can be seen as preserving the best features of the former while dispensing with what is widely regarded as its most undesirable elements. More specifically, while retaining the managerial benefits of advanced specialization and organizational meticulousness, the proactive society can be said to complement them with an emphasis put on certain traits highly reminiscent of premodern times: namely, versatility and self-sufficiency. Admittedly, in a society that has progressed beyond a certain level of economic complexity, hardly anyone can remain truly productive while operating in a self-sufficient manner, and under such circumstances, versatility is more likely than not to degenerate into mediocrity. However, it appears that in the proactive society, these two laudable though no longer feasible characteristics can be successfully substituted with their close and equally desirable proxies: flexibility and resourcefulness. In other words, in a sufficiently complex economy, it may no longer be possible to manage an isolated island of productivity, but in such an environment, it becomes all the more important to be skillful in managing one's distinct, personal structure of human capital and thereby collaborate effectively with other individuals tasked with similar requirements.

Still, being able to do so necessitates operating in a milieu characterized by specific structural and organizational features. It is to the analysis of these that I shall turn in the following section.

1.3 The structural and organizational characteristics of the proactive society

It is a fairly uncontroversial proposition that economics can be defined as the science of scarcity. Somewhat more contentiously, but perhaps far more importantly and no doubt more precisely, it can be described as the science that studies methods of dealing with the problem of scarcity not from the perspective of risk optimization or static utility maximization, but from that of bearing opportunity costs in the context of dynamic uncertainty (Salerno, 2009). In other words, it might be argued that all sound economic theorizing, let alone all reasoned economic action, displays an indispensable element of entrepreneurialism. This, in turn, might lead us to the somewhat counterintuitive conclusion that the more economically advanced, structurally complex, and organizationally sophisticated a given environment is, the more qualitatively challenging the corresponding problem of scarcity becomes, both from the theoretical and practical points of view. And insofar as economic advancement, structural complexification, and organizational sophistication are inextricably bound with proactivity, analyzing the nature of scarcity becomes particularly vital in the proactive society.

Even though, in absolute terms, the development of the proactive society makes the problem of scarcity far less acute than it would otherwise be (McCloskey, 2016), in relative terms, it makes it as pressing as ever, as the development in question goes hand in hand with goods and services becoming ever more qualitatively heterogeneous, especially insofar as they embody ever more qualitatively complex contributions of unique productive individuals (Wiśniewski, 2020). Thus, far from reducing specifically economic problems (the problems of scarcity and uncertainty) to purely technical problems (the problems of allocative optimization and risk management), the emergence of the proactive society makes the former ever more qualitatively intricate, challenging, and rewarding.

This phenomenon can be usefully illustrated by examining the self-reinforcing spiral actuated by the interdependent activities of various functional categories of entrepreneurs. In virtue of introducing all kinds of commercially viable innovations, Schumpeterian entrepreneurs in an important sense recreate the problem of scarcity in ever more challenging and intricate manifestations, whereupon Kirznerian entrepreneurs begin to tackle them, thereby clearing the ground for the emergence of additional Schumpeterian disruptions and so on (Holcombe, 2003). In other words, proactivity constitutes one of the main drivers of the never-ending chase after the unattainable horizon of economic equilibrium, with the crucial caveat being that along the way, the equilibrium in question becomes progressively more detailed in its qualitative description.

This conclusion has significant structural and organizational implications. In the previous section, I noted that proactivity can be broadly defined as the acquisition and frequent deployment of quasi-entrepreneurial skills by the majority of the workforce, including rank and file employees. A natural extension of this phenomenon appears to be a special eagerness to cross the line into the domain of full-scale entrepreneurship. And as, as per the definition adopted in the introduction of the present chapter, such entrepreneurship implies asset ownership, one of the most prominent structural and organizational characteristics of the proactive society is likely to be an exceptional proliferation of firms.

To be more precise, it is to be expected that as more and more people become accustomed to adjusting their skills and competences to the dynamically changing environment of external market data, an increasing number of them may decide to enter the profession that allows for actively shaping the environment in question. Instead of adapting their personal offers to the broader visions implemented by their bosses, they can thereby enact such visions themselves and reach their intended customers directly by means of their cognitive leadership (Witt, 2007).

A few remarks might be in order here concerning the relationship between such newly minted cognitive leaders and the inherent uncertainty of the market. It has been recently claimed that the dynamism and unpredictability of the modern global economy have given rise to a social class condemned to unprecedentedly precarious lifestyles and unsteady professional careers (Standing, 2011). In response, one might suggest that such highly general observations run the risk of conflating categorically different kinds of uncertainty. On the one hand, they could refer to the uncertainty associated with the disappearance of "lifetime jobs" and the emergence of "protean employment", which, admittedly, is a natural consequence of rapid economic development in a globalized world, but is vastly offset by the attendant prospects of rising real earnings and being able to live off of passive income. If, however, such compensatory rewards are not enough to alleviate one's anxiety in the face of this kind of uncertainty, living in a proactive society allows one to make the "final switch" and move relatively easily from the ranks of hired employees or gig contractors into the ranks of full-blooded entrepreneurs, so that one might be personally and ultimately in charge of one's professional life.

Hence, on the other hand, the above observations may also refer to the whole gamut of uncertainty types associated with assuming an active role in the entrepreneurial process (Packard, Clark, and Klein, 2017). These, one might plausibly argue, are far more demanding that their non-entrepreneurial counterparts, as dealing with them successfully requires not just adjusting one's personal human capital to the dynamically changing external structures of production but also using it to create a personal structure of production in a dynamically changing environment of external market variables. In other words, in a world characterized by fundamental uncertainty, it is impossible to eliminate the precarity of life – the most one can do in such an epistemic milieu is to choose one's preferred form of precarity, bearing in mind that the one associated with being one's own boss is much more cognitively challenging than the one associated with being someone else's employee.

That being said, widespread habituation to performing non-automatable labor, engaging in proxy-entrepreneurship, pursuing a protean career, and performing other tasks typical of membership in a proactive society are bound to make entrepreneurial precarity less intimidating or at least less misunderstood. This, in turn, as indicated earlier, is more likely than not to make the proactive society particularly heavily populated with firm owners, startup founders, and other initiative-taking asset holders.

The above conclusion is further reinforced by a number of additional considerations. In accordance with perhaps the most prevalent conception of the firm, the role of the institution in question is to reduce transaction costs (Coase, 1988: 5–7). However, some authors point out that the Coasian approach is largely an offshoot of the static general equilibrium tradition, which, by definition, dispenses with analysis of the entrepreneurial market process (Boudreaux and Holcombe, 1989a). It should be noted here that the introduction of an entrepreneurial perspective into the picture not only enlarges our understanding of the firm, which is thereby presented as a crucial institutional tool for dealing with market uncertainty, but also deepens it in virtue of "dynamizing" Coasian insights. That is to say, it brings our attention to the fact that real-world firms have to minimize not only "static" search, bargaining, and enforcement costs but their "dynamic" counterparts as well. Needless to say, in the proactive society, characterized by whimsical consumer tastes, high capital mobility, rapid technological advancement, and pervasive intercultural cross-fertilization, such dynamic transaction costs are particularly substantial. As a result, its members can be expected to rely increasingly heavily on the transactional advantages afforded by firms, especially those of the Schumpeterian variety (Langlois, 2007).

Furthermore, being responsive to rapid changes taking place in the external business environment and addressing unique entrepreneurial challenges on a continual basis require setting up sufficiently flexible and simultaneously robust governance structures. Firms are well suited to performing such a role, as they can be regarded as constitutional orders in their own right (Evans and Wenzel, 2013). It should be kept in mind that even in the proactive society, firm owners – that is, the primary exercisers of entrepreneurial judgment – must retain a considerable degree of managerial oversight. This is because even in a highly decentralized decision-making milieu, they still need to provide their subordinates with a requisite level of strategic guidance, macro-scale coordination, and responsiveness to time-sensitive issues (Foss and Klein, 2014). Thus, their partial delegation of judgment to their employees should be seen as going hand in hand with creating the kind of business habitat where the latter can successfully deploy their proxy-entrepreneurial potential. In other words, it might be said that even in the proactive society, bosses still have to boss their subordinates around, but in a more indirect, rule-setting manner, which belongs to a higher level in the institutional structure of production (Coase, 1992; Williamson, 2000). To do that effectively, however, they need to avail themselves of the organizational capacity of firms and be particularly eager to utilize its constitutional dimension.

Finally, as flourishing in the proactive society requires combining professional specialization with organizational versatility, it goes without saying that its successful members should be thought of as possessors of highly specific assets that comprise their individual structures of human capital. Consequently, one can expect them to operate in an environment that is heavily populated by firms understood as vehicles for solving the holdup problem (Riordan and Williamson, 1985). More specifically, it is to be anticipated that in the proactive society, such individuals are bound either to become full-fledged entrepreneurs or to be offered exclusive full-time employment (instead of being hired on more flexible terms) so that their highly specialized skills and competences become strictly associated with particular enterprises. In sum, employment in the proactive society appears likely to present an unusual combination of diachronic flexibility and synchronic stability – that is to say, it is likely to necessitate being ready to work for multiple employers over the course of one's career while simultaneously guaranteeing that at any given stage of one's career, one can enjoy solid and close-knit relations with a single employer.

All of the foregoing observations suggest that the institution of the firm assumes particular prominence and importance in the organizational structure of the proactive society. However, in response, one might argue that such insights are not especially illuminating, as they apply equally well to the managerial society. Why, then, one might ask, should they be regarded as testifying to the supposed exceptional entrepreneurialism and decision-making decentralization of the former?

In answering this question, one should point out that, as mentioned earlier, the proactive society should not be thought of as simply elevating the importance of the firm but also as encouraging the numerical proliferation of this institution. This conclusion follows naturally from the assumption that the social model under consideration puts a particular premium on entrepreneurial and proxy-entrepreneurial skills. If the former are to be leveraged by a growing number of individuals, the number of individually owned firms needs to grow accordingly, and even the latter cannot be meaningfully developed in an economy dominated by a limited coterie of bureaucratized corporate monoliths. As, however, it is conceptually inconceivable that widespread firm ownership could go together with increasing business consolidation, the proactive society is bound to be "structurally entrepreneurial" (Klein, 2008: 176–177), that is, composed of a uniquely large number of small business entities.

This contention can be elaborated on the basis of all of the more specific points raised in the preceding paragraphs. First of all, an economy characterized by rapid technological development and substantial capital mobility is one in which the holdup problem is solvable by means other than vertical integration, such as reliance on cheap long-distance transportation to obtain otherwise inaccessible specific assets or manufacturing their substitutes by utilizing technological innovations. Consequently, the proactive society, which by definition exhibits all of the above features, is likely to display tendencies toward deconsolidation and de-verticalization, that is, toward reduction in firm size and increase in firm number (Langlois, 2003).

Second, as ever more employees become accustomed to performing proxy-entrepreneurial tasks, the ranks of full-fledged entrepreneurs are bound to grow correspondingly. As, however, entrepreneurs by definition head companies instead of working for them in a subordinate manner, in the conditions under consideration, their pool of potential employees inevitably shrinks. This, especially in connection with the aforementioned processes of corporate de-concentration, leads to the conclusion that in the proactive society, the average number of employees per company is likely to be considerably smaller than in its more managerially oriented counterparts.

Third, operating one's enterprise successfully in a world of substantial dynamic transaction costs requires staying abreast of large amounts of information that is simultaneously highly contextual and rapidly mutable. In such an environment, transactional economies of scale become quickly overtaken by organizational diseconomies of scale (McAfee and McMillan, 1995). Furthermore, markets for highly specialized intellectual capital, whose widespread existence is characteristic of the proactive society, are by definition comparatively thin and illiquid and thus easily monopolizable. However, given the fact that becoming the exclusive user of a nonspecific factor of production short-circuits one's ability to engage in meaningful economic calculation (Klein, 1996), and operating in such markets effectively necessitates refraining from the pursuit of a monopolistic position. This is especially so in view of the uniquely broad non-specificity of intellectual capital and the corresponding severity of not being able to assess the opportunity costs of using it.

Finally, creating constitutional orders in which novel goods and services can be skillfully developed and novel managerial challenges successfully confronted requires infusing them with a requisite degree of "institutional stickiness" (Boettke, Coyne, and Leeson, 2008). That is to say, such orders should be "indigenous" and "endogenous" in their orientation: on the one hand recognized as being consistent with the authentic values held by employees, and on the other hand capable of being meaningfully cocreated by them. In the absence of such features, they are unlikely to attract collaborators equipped with skills necessary to flourish in the proactive society.

By the same token, the organizational structures in question have to be comparatively small, as otherwise they run the risk of becoming too alienating to employees with strong and specific value orientations and too unwieldy to allow for their collaborative, bottom-up development. Thus, in addition to confronting the standard calculation problem mentioned in the preceding paragraph, overly large firms and bloated systems of corporate governance may need to confront an even more demanding challenge while operating in the proactive society: that of calculating prospective profits and losses in terms of strictly implicit values associated with highly specific forms of intellectual capital. Making the constitutional arrangements of business entities institutionally sticky appears to be the most promising solution in this connection, as it allows for effectively eliciting tacit employee knowledge, which provides an indispensable basis for evaluating the relevant implicit costs and benefits (Intan-Soraya and Chew, 2010).

In conclusion, the proactive society can be justifiably regarded as being not only uniquely entrepreneurial in its approach toward problem-solving but also as singularly capable of "democratizing" entrepreneurialism in the dual sense of rapidly growing the ranks of business owners and multiplying the number of non-owning employees promoted to genuinely discretionary positions. This may be seen as a particularly attractive combination insofar as it enables the overall organizational structure of society to grow in complexity – thus presumably making it increasingly efficient in terms of advancing large-scale social cooperation – while simultaneously making individual segments of the structure in question maximally lean, participatory, and non-bureaucratic. Nonetheless, it should be kept in mind that such an arrangement can arise, let alone flourish, only if all of the parties involved commit themselves to the entrepreneurial ethos and do not taint it by resorting to clientelist practices.

That is to say, while all of the foregoing considerations refer to the possibilities and constraints that firms have to face in the proactive society qua business entities, it cannot be discounted that they may try to bolster the former and circumvent the latter by assuming the additional identity of rent-seekers and political lobbyists. For instance, by ensuring its access to subsidies and securing a political grant of monopoly privilege, a company may grow beyond the maximum size sustainable in the proactive society and retain market dominance. This is because by engaging in "political entrepreneurship" (McCaffrey and Salerno, 2011), the company in question may absorb the total supply of intellectual capital specific to its industry while externalizing the losses associated with its inability to evaluate the alternative uses of such capital.

However, the danger described above may be more of a theoretical than a practical issue, as it is reasonable to assume that a genuinely proactive society can emerge only in an environment that is highly depoliticized and, thus, mostly resistant to rent-seeking and other forms of market distortion brought about by the commingling of business and politics. It is to the exploration of the reasons behind this contention that I intend to turn in the following section.

1.4 The political characteristics of the proactive society

If the proactive society is to be defined as a communal environment characterized by a particularly pronounced level of personal initiative, individual dynamism, organizational elasticity, and responsiveness to rapidly changing conditions, it might seem that the politicization of life, including especially bureaucratic sprawl, is directly antagonistic toward its core values. After all, the so-called political means, in contrast to the economic means – as described, for example, in the classical study by Oppenheimer (1922) – can be defined in terms of coercive monopolization, imposed hierarchization, and procedural rigidity, which are features completely alien to the spirit of proactivity.

This is particularly so if the political means are to be thought of as the ones utilized in the context of so-called representative politics, where direct self-governance is replaced with what is often little more than rubber stamping the agendas of fossilized party systems. Furthermore, the self-serving character of political decision-making of the representative kind is additionally compounded by the institutional logic whereby power is increasingly vested in intergovernmental organizations, international bureaucracies, and other entities whose members are elected indirectly at best (Hülsmann, 1997). Needless to say, in such a situation, the individual is as deprived of the ability to exercise proactive self-governance as is humanly conceivable in a non-dictatorial environment.

Thus, it is reasonable to assume that the emergence of the proactive society would require a substantial depoliticization of world affairs or – to put the matter somewhat more technically – their thoroughgoing decentralization, horizontalization, and genuine contractualization. As the economic and social realm is intimately entangled with the political realm (Wagner, 2014), especially in today's globalized world of complex and oftentimes opaque organizational interrelations, accomplishing the goal in question may appear to be an insurmountable challenge. However, what I shall argue in the following paragraphs is that there are at least two major propulsive forces operating in the present situation that may break the political crust that prevents the proactive society from assuming its full and robust form.

First, as indicated earlier, it is simply impossible for today's global intricate socioeconomic order to retain its operational efficiency in the context of ever-increasing politicization, bureaucratization, and upward regulatory harmonization (Gwartney, Lawson, and Holcombe, 1999; Bjørnskov and Foss, 2008). Thus, if the world is to continue enjoying the considerable benefits afforded by the currently existing semi-proactive and semi-managerial society, its inhabitants have to at least restrain the politico-bureaucratic affinities of its latter part, even if they are not yet ready to promote actively the uncompromisingly decentralist and entrepreneurial features of its former part. And second, the active promotion in question may well become increasingly pronounced as more and more people discover the unique opportunities of the proactive approach and reflect on the political conditions under which such an approach can flourish.

Let me then begin by discussing in greater detail the first category of the abovementioned phenomena, that is, the one associated with the fundamental incompatibility between proactivity and politicization.

First, it goes without saying that in a world progressively reliant on non-automatable labor, proxy entrepreneurship, and the successful pursuit of protean careers, the quantity and quality of information needed for efficient large-scale cooperation grow ever larger and more complex. By the same token, as suggested in the previous section, the discretionary competences of individual employees and their spontaneous groupings need to grow accordingly if the relevant informational challenges are to be met successfully. The same goes for the ability of individuals to move around the world freely in search of the most promising career options, especially in an environment where such opportunities shift around at a rapid pace.

In this connection, one should keep in mind that even in the managerial society, the amount of contextual and tacit information is far too high to allow for its efficient centralized administration, which forms the basis for the understanding of market competition as a crucial discovery procedure (Hayek, 2002). Thus, freedom from attempts at the bureaucratic planning of economic systems becomes even more essential in the proactive society. This goes both for the operation of firms, which need to be maximally flexible in experimenting with incentive structures aimed at dredging up latent employee potential, and for the activities of individuals, who need to be maximally flexible in traversing the world in pursuit of those places where their human capital will be optimally allocated. This observation is all the more important, given the fact that political interventionism tends to generate a self-reinforcing spiral of systemic crises and their counter-effective solutions (Higgs, 1987; Ikeda, 1997), which can not only quell the development of economic and social proactivity but even cause it to retrogress.

Second, a business environment characterized by volatile consumer tastes, substantial capital mobility, quick technological advancement, and ubiquitous intercultural dealings requires firms to create organizational frameworks that are much more minutely tailored to their specific areas of specialization than those imposed by traditional political institutions in a one-size-fits-all manner. Thus, the role of special economic zones, charter cities, private neighborhood associations, and other forms of truly contractual governance (Boudreaux and Holcombe, 1989b) becomes particularly salient under such conditions. This is especially so in view of the tendency of political decision-making to lag behind the problems generated on a continuous basis by the process of economic development and transactional complexification (Stringham, 2015).

In other words, a far-reaching depoliticization of socioeconomic affairs – or, if one prefers, their comprehensive contractualization – appears to be a crucial prerequisite for firms being able to serve as functional constitutional orders. And, as noted above and in the previous section, they have to be able to serve as such if they are to allow for the successful transition to the proactive society and for the successful tackling of its distinct challenges.

Third, it has been long recognized that large-scale social cooperation cannot thrive in the absence of robust bonds of trust (Fukuyama, 1996). This observation becomes particularly noteworthy in the context of fostering phenomena that require proactivity such as direct client interaction, proxy-entrepreneurship, and organizational elasticity. Meanwhile, politicization can be regarded as the prime manifestation of institutionalized distrust, insofar as it necessarily involves ever-expanding measures of coercion and restriction. By the same token, it can be seen as a singularly potent source of institutionalized moral hazard. More specifically, as the deployment of the political means brings about a forced separation of ownership and control with respect to privately held assets (Hülsmann, 2006), it generates the perpetual threat of losing control over one's resources and the corresponding willingness to treat every member of society as a potential rent-seeker.

Furthermore, politicization promotes the so-called regime uncertainty (Higgs, 1997) – that is, it makes the legal and regulatory framework within which entrepreneurial activities take place unpredictable and arbitrarily mutable. As a result, not only do interpersonal relations of trust break down, but respect for the law is eroded as well.

Thus, one may conclude that the only viable way of securing general social trust and legal functionality under conditions that call for proactivity is to push for legal polycentricity and organizational self-governance. This, one might argue, is the sole feasible method of ensuring that the law is simultaneously stable, transparent, and commonsensical enough to command general respect and flexible enough to encourage trusting relations even in highly novel, complex, and context-specific situations (Leeson and Coyne, 2012). Needless to say, this point ties in naturally with the previously discussed issue of the role of firms as autonomous constitutional orders.

Finally, inasmuch as proactivity can be closely linked with entrepreneurialism, it must be noticed that the formal essence of the entrepreneurial relation is its strictly contractual character. In other words, the relation in question is, in normative terms, strictly symmetrical, horizontal, and egalitarian. Political arrangements, on the other hand, are necessarily asymmetrical, vertical, and hierarchical in their nature insofar as they divide society into rulers and ruled, which is inevitably the case even in their most participatory form. When viewed through the lens of sufficiently consistent ethical principles, such arrangements may be reasonably regarded as based on double moral standards, which endow monopolistic apparatuses of violence with broad and ultimately unjustifiable privileges (Huemer, 2013). Hence, in a society whose members are increasingly accustomed to being active negotiators of contracts, such double moral standards may become progressively unacceptable.

In response to all of the above observations, one might suggest that no matter how desirable depoliticization might be in the context of stimulating proactivity, it is in the nature of politics that it does not yield to even the most socially beneficial phenomena if they are to diminish the influence of entrenched power groups. However, even if one were to concede the fundamental correctness of this suggestion, it does not follow that oligarchic plotting is always destined to triumph over entrepreneurial emancipation, especially if proactively disposed individuals understand the inherent logic of the former (Salerno, 2008).

This is where the second of the previously mentioned propulsive forces conducive to breaking through the politico-bureaucratic fossilization of the present socioeconomic order comes into the picture. More specifically, it can be argued that the same phenomena that require ever greater proactivity on the part of ordinary members of society also naturally nudge them in the direction of increased understanding of the unique advantages of adopting a self-starting and forward-looking attitude. This, in turn, might induce them to agitate for the kind of political changes or undertake the kind of self-organizing endeavors that allow the fruits of such an attitude to flourish. Let us now discuss some of the more concrete examples of how such a process might manifest itself.

First, greater demand for non-automatable labor might result in greater political consciousness, reduced susceptibility to populism, and other developments conducive to augmenting the popularity of self-governance as compared with representative politics. This is because, as indicated in Section 1.2 of the present chapter, automation necessitates a shift in the labor market toward specifically human-centric tasks, whose successful completion requires advanced psychological, communicational, and interpersonal skills. Needless to say, these may prove crucial in resisting the debilitating influence of rational ignorance (Somin, 2013), rational irrationality (Caplan, 2011), passivity in the face of financial cronyism (Stockman, 2013), and other phenomena indicative of one's perceived helplessness against established power structures.

Second, the widespread advent of proxy-entrepreneurship might engender greater desire for self-governance in view of its connection with highly decentralized modes of organization. That is to say, insofar as proxy-entrepreneurs are expected to anticipate and address unique problems without deferring to their superiors in the chain of command, they might become increasingly unwilling to tolerate politicians, let alone unelected bureaucrats, making decisions on their behalf without their direct consent. In other words, they might be particularly eager to exercise the "voice" option and work toward the establishment of conditions under which such voice can be heard especially resoundingly. It is worth noting that an environment of unshackled entrepreneurial initiative might be seen as ideal in this context, as entrepreneurship can be regarded as the essential bridge between word and action, where the latter speaks far louder than the former (Wiśniewski, 2019).

Finally, the growing role of protean careers goes hand in hand with an increasing premium placed on labor mobility, which, in turn, is likely to raise the awareness of laborers concerning the value of the "exit" option. That is to say, as career seekers become steadily more accustomed to changing their place of occupation on a routine basis, they might become progressively more adept at utilizing the power of boycott, ostracism, blackballing, voting with one's feet, etc., especially as directed against unsatisfactory political, legal, and regulatory arrangements. By the same token, they might provide a pressing rationale for thoroughgoing political decentralization and regional autonomization, whereby individual communities are able to offer organizational and administrative solutions tailored to the demands of specific social groups (Cséfalvay, 2011), including those defined primarily by their professional identity.

It is worth noting that all of the aforementioned phenomena have significant potential to strengthen the most formidable of decentralist forces – namely, secessionism. In addition, it appears a reasonable assumption that the combined influence of increased political consciousness and an amplified reliance on the voice and exit options can give secessionism two mutually reinforcing forms: active and passive. By the former, I mean direct political engagement aimed at gaining autonomy for local communities and the territories inhabited by them, whereas by the latter, I mean initiating migration movements geared toward changing the ideological preferences of specific populations and subsequently modifying the local laws in the desired direction. Taken together, both of these forms may provide crucial impetus for the kind of political proactivity that paves the ground for subsequent proactivity in other areas of large-scale social cooperation, capable of reaching its full potential under favorable "constitutional" conditions.

In conclusion, the present world appears to be burdened by a tension between, on the one hand, the dynamizing influence of technological progress, organizational complexification, and capital mobility and, on the other hand, the deadening influence of international bureaucratization, regulatory opaqueness, and administrative centralization. While the former both results from and engenders proactivity, the latter both reflects and perpetuates a lack thereof. And while it might seem that the logic of collective action naturally favors the triumph of the latter (Olson, 1971), one must never forget that it is ultimately ideas and preferences, not institutional path dependency or structural inertia, that determine the course of social development (Stringham and Hummel, 2010).

In this connection, I noted that progressing beyond a critical threshold of work automation, task specialization, and occupational elasticity is likely to result in an increased understanding of the political preconditions of the emergence of a flourishing proactive society. This, in turn, may generate the momentum necessary to overcome the initiative-stifling impact of bureaucratic sprawl and decision-making exclusion. If, however, the momentum in question is to be sufficiently persistent and clear-sighted, it must be deeply internalized on the ethical level and grounded in firm moral principles. It is these issues that will be the focus of the next section.

1.5 The ethical characteristics of the proactive society

As I indicated in the introduction, the analytical approach employed throughout the present book relies primarily on the insights of economics. As such, it is firmly committed to the principle of value freedom, that is, to describing the causal laws that govern the cooperative logic of the proactive society, without suggesting that this particular socioeconomic system is objectively desirable and indisputably superior to its managerial, feudal, or primitivist alternative.

However, normative considerations necessarily enter into the investigation at hand in an oblique manner. That is to say, it can be plausibly argued that the organizational and political characteristics of the proactive society described in the preceding sections cannot emerge, let alone persist, in the absence of an appropriate ethical culture. In other words, moral values, virtues, and dispositions provide a crucial bedrock for the analysis of broader structures of social cooperation while keeping it strictly positive, as value freedom need not imply value independence.

To take a concrete example, the spectacular economic development spurred by the outbreak of the Industrial Revolution was caused directly by the unprecedented degree of capital accumulation and the attendant outburst of innovation, but these phenomena were, in turn, crucially conditioned by the preceding changes in the prevailing moral culture. More specifically, productivity-enhancing commercial activities began to flourish when the entrepreneurial class was accorded a dignified social status (McCloskey, 2010). By extension, it seems reasonable to suggest that a similar shift in normative attitudes and dispositional evaluations would have to take place if a solid moral foundation for the emergence of a mature proactive society were to be established. By the same token, the process under consideration would have to be accompanied by an increasing premium put on the acquisition of appropriate values and virtues. Let us now analyze their character in more detail.

First, as I have pointed out repeatedly in the previous sections, progressing work automation is bound to grow the demand for inherently human-centric kinds of labor. This, almost by definition, is highly likely to make the bulk of the relevant tasks morally sensitive on account of their subject-, not object-related nature. Put another way, while working primarily or solely with machines does not require any extensive ethical competences, interacting primarily or solely with one's fellow human beings clearly does. This is especially so insofar as automation continues to subsume not only purely mechanical tasks but also those occupations that involve only a low degree of human engagement and limited interpersonal complexity. Thus, even rank and file employees who engage with customers and other relevant parties can be increasingly expected to display not simply rote courtesy but also genuine kindness and helpfulness aimed at solving unique, agent-specific problems.

This, of course, requires not just narrowly conceived professional competence, but proactivity as well, whereby one is willing to subject one's occupational skills to constant on-the-job self-development. Such development, in turn, necessitates acquiring and cultivating the virtue of courage, which allows for confronting singular, previously unencountered business situations, and as such is an essential component of moral intelligence (Lee and Elliott-Lee, 2006). Furthermore, courage, understood as the golden mean between timidity and rashness, enables projecting well-founded confidence, which is an indispensable tool for building customer trust, and which cannot be replaced by impersonal, introspectively empty guarantees generated by machines.

Second, the advent of proxy-entrepreneurship and the corresponding extension of the discretionary competencies of nonexecutive employees opens up a broad space not just for proactive problem-solving but for managerial moral hazard as well. This conclusion follows naturally from the fact that proxy-entrepreneurs operate neither under the disciplining constraints of asset ownership nor under any hierarchically verifiable criteria of technical performance. Consequently, their professional discipline has to derive from sources that are strictly internal, not external. If, however, such discipline is not to stunt the resourcefulness and ingenuity characteristic of the proactive orientation, it needs to be rooted not in mere respect for occupational conventions, but in firmly grounded moral virtues, chief among them being the virtue of temperance (Warren, 1994).

In this context, temperance can be regarded as the middle ground between the submissive inertia typical of unambitious low-level employees and the swashbuckling bravado of arrogant executives determined to get rich quickly, no matter the cost to the long-run prospects of the companies they work for. Subjecting one's proxy-entrepreneurial competencies to the requirements of this virtue may result not only in the elimination of moral hazard but also in aligning one's long-term career trajectory with the long-term strategic vision of one's employer, thereby further reinforcing one's commitment to sensible risk management and supervisory integrity. Thus, temperance emerges as the crucial trait of character that allows for subordinating the dynamism of proactivity to the calmness of responsibility.

Finally, the ever more likely prospect of having to pursue a protean career forces non-entrepreneurs to exhibit certain essential elements of entrepreneurial thinking in dealing with their individual productive assets, material and nonmaterial alike. More specifically, instead of reactively adjusting their talents, skills, and other marketable qualities to the preexisting capital structure of production, they need to be willing to co-create the structure in question by proactively offering firm owners their unique competitive advantages. If, however, the activity under consideration is not to degenerate into empty peddling and haphazard grandstanding, it has to be underpinned by the pivotal commercial virtue of prudence (Machan, 2009).

As prudence is the virtue that allows its possessor to identify extremes that thwart the acquisition of other virtues, it can be rightly seen as a vital instrument for navigating the two issues mentioned in the preceding paragraphs as well. That is to say, employees habituated to switching between careers by definition display the kind of courage that is required to confront a variety of distinct professional settings. Consequently, even if some of those settings do not involve frequent interpersonal contacts, their heterogeneity by itself can provide a good grounding in dealing with the realm of true uncertainty – that is, with the domain of unknown unknowns penetrable by human foresight, but not by pre-programmed algorithmic instructions (Engelhardt, 2013).

Likewise, being accustomed to combining specialization and versatility – that is, being ready to juggle disparate occupations while leveraging their productive synergies – can prove to be instrumental in giving one's career the long-term orientation, reminiscent of the strategies adopted by seasoned entrepreneurs (Pellegrini and Ciappei, 2015). Such an orientation can be said to embody the virtue of temperance insofar as it helps to avoid intertemporal miscoordination in managing one's personal structure of human capital. More specifically, it can help prevent situations where one takes up a well-paying job that is completely out of tune with one's distinct talents and interests, only to be laid off shortly afterwards due to labor market fluctuations and realize that the job in question provided one with no genuine opportunities for professional development needed for transitioning to another gainful occupation. Such a scenario can be said to involve an instance of intertemporal mismanagement inasmuch as it increases one's short-run gains at the expense of depleting one's long-run productive potential, temperance being the virtue that guards against making such errors and prudence being the virtue that allows for identifying situations in which such errors may arise and be particularly damaging.

While all of the above observations pertain to the moral assets whose acquisition may be especially desirable in the proactive society as far as employees are concerned, a similar analysis can be applied to employers as well.

First, a plausible psychological expectation grounded in the mature version of Maslow's hierarchy of needs (Koltko-Rivera, 2006) suggests that as economic development progresses, customers are increasingly likely to demand goods and services that are not only cheaper, more abundant, and more easily accessible but also ever more qualitatively satisfying. To put the matter in more conventionally economic nomenclature, it stands to reason that the law of diminishing marginal utility applies not only to specific classes of goods understood in narrowly utilitarian terms but also to broader categories of goods understood in more robustly normative terms. That is to say, satiation with "conspicuous consumption" brought about by rapid enrichment may well result in customers becoming more ethically fastidious – not necessarily on account of any suddenly discovered ethical sensitivity, but simply due to a surfeit of "mere utility". This, in turn, may create a business environment in which proactivity is inextricably linked with the ability to deploy moral imagination and avoid "moral myopia" (Drumwright and Murphy, 2004), that is, the ability to anticipate morally laden consumer demands and respond to them in a genuine manner that goes way beyond ethical window dressing.

Second, as the proactive society places a growing premium on entrepreneurial skills, its emergence goes hand in hand with an increase in the number of firm owners, that is, those individuals who naturally progress from the rank of proxy-entrepreneurs to the rank of their full-blooded counterparts. This implies that in order to stand out from this increasingly large crowd, entrepreneurs are likely to succeed insofar as they are willing to differentiate their selling propositions in qualitative terms from those of their competitors. In this connection, utilizing so-called strategic corporate social responsibility (Porter and Kramer, 2006) might turn out to be particularly beneficial. However, one should bear in mind that leveraging this strategy successfully requires being serious about one's normative commitments instead of treating them as a pure marketing ploy, as an ethically fastidious customer is likely to be accustomed to evaluating the results of one's entrepreneurial vision rather than the stated intentions behind its pursuit.

What can plausibly further enhance the above reorientation is the fact that in a progressively wealthier world, businesspeople can be increasingly expected to regard entrepreneurship as not just a tool for material enrichment but also as a means of normative improvement through unique value creation (Manish and Sutter, 2016). One should hasten to add, however, that adopting such an extended conception of business success can by no means imply losing sight of the overarching commercial goal of profit making, lest entrepreneurship be deprived of its distinct character and unique wealth-building power. In other words, the conception in question, instead of dethroning profit making as the ultimate objective of entrepreneurial activity, consists in pointing out that, especially in a society of ethically choosy individuals, profitability can be seen as proof of achieving a number of additional objectives, including those that go beyond the satisfaction of purely subjective consumer preferences.

Third, the emergence of ever more complex forms of corporate organization requires a growing reliance on proxy-entrepreneurship, and, as hinted at earlier, proxy-entrepreneurship is unlikely to devolve into creative rent-seeking only in organizational structures imbued with the spirit of authentic ethical commitment. Building such structures successfully calls for experimenting with various combinations of ethical capital, capable of actualizing various complementary organizational virtues, but no such experimentation can work out well if business owners are unable to identify prospective employees who possess or can be induced to develop such virtues. Thus, as one of the core components of exercising entrepreneurial judgment is making sound decisions about the decision-making capacity of others (Emmett, 2011), deploying such judgment effectively in an environment where hired workers are endowed with extensive discretionary competences demands particular sensitivity to their explicit and latent moral qualities.

Fourth, technological development allows for devising methods of unifying various hitherto supposedly opposed economic categories such as production and consumption or work and leisure. To take some concrete examples, the so-called sharing economy enables the functional transformation of consumer goods such as cars and private apartments into factors of production such as ridesharing vehicles and rental living space. Likewise, apparently leisurely online chess games played by employees during work breaks can help them replenish their productive power, thereby turning out to be an efficiency-enhancing tool rather than a reluctantly accepted drain on performance. In order, however, to make effective use of such categorial syntheses, entrepreneurs need to exhibit heightened moral imagination and systems thinking (Werhane, 2002), whereby seemingly conflicting values can be harmonized when viewed as elements of a more deeply interrelated whole.

Finally, entrepreneurship can be justifiably regarded as a profession whose practitioners are singularly required to confront and resolve value conflicts on a regular basis, which is an essential element of their directive role in the world of scarcity and uncertainty. Needless to say, a prominent place among such conflicts is held by moral dilemmas, that is, situations in which every conceivable choice is bound to transgress an important moral value or frustrate a significant moral rule. In the context of business, such dilemmas may involve, for example, choosing between the utilitarian goals of expanding one's enterprise globally in order to reach as many customers as possible with affordable products and the deontological goals of keeping one's enterprise focused on the needs of the local, close-knit community out of which it grew. What may complicate making such decisions is the fact that, as illustrated by the example in question, it is far from being obvious which of the available options in a given morally dilemmatic scenario is more promising from a purely commercial point of view. This, again, underscores the degree to which economic and ethical considerations are tightly interconnected and oftentimes mutually reinforcing in spite of their fundamental categorial differences.

In view of the above, entrepreneurship can be rightly seen as a paradigmatic area where practical wisdom is exercised by means of employing resources offered by various ethical theories and attempting to reconcile their prescriptions on a case-by-case basis. By the same token, it can be seen as an essential real-world example of a field where complex moral solutions are successfully implemented despite there being no ethical "master principle" capable of covering every conceivable dilemmatic scenario (Arnold, Audi, and Zwolinski, 2010).

In sum, full-blooded entrepreneurship and its proxy version and other occupations grounded in proactivity both require the emergence of an appropriate ethical culture and serve as a training ground for the relevant moral virtues. As, however, developing and internalizing such virtues demand intellectual discipline and discerning focus, it seems reasonable to suggest that the ethical framework described in the present section would have to be combined with an accompanying cognitive framework if the proactive society were to assume a sufficiently robust form. This suggestion shall be explored in greater detail in the next section.

1.6 The cognitive characteristics of the proactive society

As proactivity involves acting in advance of future contingencies and implementing solutions on one's own initiative, it is clearly a characteristic whose possession implies intellectual independence and cognitive dynamism. One should be wary, however, of concluding on the basis of this observation that prospering in a proactive society requires above-average cognitive potential. Instead, it appears far more accurate to suggest that it requires reorienting the potential in question toward specific functions whose development is typically stunted in a strictly managerial model of organization.

To understand this contention better, it is worthwhile to begin by reflecting critically on the well-worn notion of the "information society" (Webster, 2014). At first glance, it might seem that the proactive society and the information society are simply two different descriptions of the same overall phenomenon, where informational multiplicity and complexity call for the rapid acquisition and processing of relevant signals, one's cognitive ability being directly correlated with the efficiency of performing this task. In fact, however, the situation is far less obvious.

First and foremost, it should be noted that in the age of widespread automation and vast computing power, gathering data and assembling it into information are no longer activities that necessitate the presence of a human intellect. Furthermore, it turns out that the activity under consideration is actually profoundly nonintellectual in its mechanical repetitiveness, and, if left entirely to unthinking machines, it can easily result in creating a pervasive environment of information overload (Bawden and Robinson, 2021). Hence, it transpires that what matters in this context is not "quantitative" cognition, that is, the rapidity of collecting and processing raw data, but its qualitative counterpart, that is, the ability to select, interpret, extrapolate, and creatively build upon unfiltered streams of facts and figures. In other words, it takes specifically human, non-algorithmic judgment to transform information into knowledge or – better still – knowledge into wisdom, thus usefully applying general data patterns to concrete situations and singular cases.

An often-underappreciated insight that allows for realizing the above point more fully consists in grasping the dual informational nature of market prices and entrepreneurial competition. In this connection, the free enterprise system is typically regarded primarily as a vast, decentralized generator of signals that indicate the relative scarcity of particular goods and services on a continual basis, thereby enabling businesspeople to make sound decisions (Kirzner, 1997). However, the essential thing to notice here is that successful entrepreneurs are not those who passively absorb as much market-generated information as possible, but those who actively select only that information that seems promising in making accurate forward-looking analyses. After all, even the most "efficient" market is only as capable of continuously harmonizing supply and demand as those of its participants endowed with the rare ability of converting publicly available "objective" data into far-sighted subjective expectations (Campos Dias de Sousa and Howden, 2015). Those, on the other hand, who succumb to information overload and consequently make decisions in the dark are penalized by losses and are eventually removed from the entrepreneurial role (Mises, 2008).

Thus, insofar as the automation of routine procedures consistently pushes even rank and file workers in the direction of ineradicably human-centric tasks, and insofar as such tasks involve a prominent entrepreneurial (or at least quasi-entrepreneurial) component, flourishing in the proactive society requires a "negative" and "qualitative" reorientation in one's cognitive competences. In other words, it requires the ability to filter out the mass of information whose cognitive value is low, nonexistent, or negative and the corresponding ability to fish out rare pieces of information whose cognitive value is substantial. To illustrate the approach in question on the basis of a simple example, an employee of a human resources department who evaluates CVs and cover letters should be able to sift out irrelevant, platitudinous, and self-aggrandizing remarks while focusing on indications of genuine productivity, even if the latter are not in tune with any bureaucratically prescribed scripts. That is to say, the employee under consideration should know in any given situation which features to make absent from the relevant specification (Long, 2006).

Second, as soon as firms become sufficiently large, specialized, and organizationally intricate, no singular controlling entity can centralize the information needed to manage such business structures effectively. Hence, broad discretionary competences need to be given to proxy-entrepreneurs, including those that empower them to establish independent information channels. However, it must be noted that the elevation of regular employees into the ranks of proxy-entrepreneurs crucially changes the character of their informational tasks: instead of routinely processing data that feed into conventional models and predictable systems, they need to be able to imagine hitherto unencountered configurations of data and creatively interact with their actual manifestations. Most notably, when required to cooperate with clients, suppliers, subcontractors, and other relevant parties, they need to exhibit "emphatic accuracy" (McMullen, 2015), that is, the cognitive ability to establish stable collaborative networks in the process of identifying and exploiting value propositions.

The emphatic nature of the ability in question implies that, in informational terms, deploying it successfully necessitates utilizing contextual and tacit knowledge (Oguz and Sengun, 2011) – that is, the kind of knowledge that stems from individual proactive insight and thus cannot be accumulated and disseminated through any formal data management plan. From this, it follows that in the proactive society, the main cognitive task of higher-level managers is to display higher-order emphatic accuracy, that is, the capacity to create organizational environments that are naturally conducive to the elicitation of contextual and tacit knowledge in their subordinates. In other words, their role is not to provide their subordinates with as great a quantity of relevant information as possible, but to institute professional frameworks in which the latter can filter the information under consideration through their unique qualitative judgments.

The above strategy might be said to embody the principles of "lean management" as applied to the issue of information overload (Brennan, 2011).

More specifically, it involves making general workplace routines as standardized and as predictable as possible in order to avoid time waste, while allowing maximum flexibility within those routines in order to encourage employee self-reliance and problem-solving creativity. That is to say, it consists of establishing "cognitive orders" designed to stimulate not so much the acquisition and storage of data, but rather its prudent selection, interpretation, and application. Within such orders, even lowest-level workers should be able to learn how to deal with analysis paralysis, make use of bounded rationality, see through framing effects, and develop other essential skills that aid informational discernment.

Finally, the advent of protean careers necessitates being able to process job market data in a particularly perceptive manner. This is because committing oneself to a suboptimal professional choice in a world where a number of such choices have to be made over the course of one's occupational career involves substantial sunk costs. Such costs need not be exceptionally bothersome in a managerial society characterized by stable, lifelong jobs, as under such conditions, establishing oneself in a given profession is likely to generate a lifetime of secure earnings. In a protean job market, on the other hand, finding oneself in a rapidly disappearing industry may trigger a sunk cost fallacy in the form of organizational continuance commitment, whereby one is unwilling to abandon the skills and competences one has already gained and move on to build new expertise from scratch (Cho and Huang, 2012: 37).

Thus, in such an environment, it becomes imperative to make professional choices that allow for acquiring skills and competences that are highly transferable across disciplines and occupations. Obviously enough, such decisions include an essential speculative dimension, meaning that their success is primarily a function not of the accumulated information concerning the available job offers, but of their careful qualitative evaluation. In other words, the facile assumption that in a globalized and dynamic world, it is easier to launch satisfying long-term professional careers on account of the widespread availability of relevant data has to be qualified by pointing to the importance of filtering such data through the judgment of long-term adaptability.

A more general implication of the above observations is that in a proactive society, learning exclusively on the basis of the standard trial-and-error formula may be prohibitively costly, especially with regard to temporal resources. While such a formula is clearly a significant tool in the mental toolkit of a proactively oriented individual, it has to be supplemented with entrepreneurial foresight grounded in the calculation of prospective opportunity costs if one is to avoid a protracted series of personal capital malinvestments capable of eliminating a poor career builder from the labor market altogether. That is to say, an effective acquisition of information in the proactive society requires a particular appreciation of the fact that assessing the optimality of any given choice must be grounded not only in temporal but in counterfactual analysis as well (Hülsmann, 2003).

More specifically, while, for instance, switching to a better-paying job might be considered as a successful move from the absolute standpoint expressed in monetary terms, the crucial question to ask in this connection is whether it is also a successful move from a relative standpoint, that is, as compared with the unrealized alternatives. After all, earning a higher salary in a new job might be a simple corollary of working in a growing economy, which implies no special entrepreneurial perspicacity on the part of a given agent. By the same token, patting oneself on the back for one's supposed career advancement while simply going with the flow of general economic growth makes one completely unprepared for going back to square one as soon as the economy enters a serious recession together with the attendant shaking up of the overall structure of production.

Professional advancement understood in counterfactual terms, on the other hand, indicates a genuine proactive orientation. This is because thinking in terms of unrealized alternatives belongs to the same cognitive category as entrepreneurial anticipation (Gaglio, 2004), whereby, instead of "going with the flow", one consciously shapes its direction or selects its most promising branch. Thus, perhaps the most unmistakable indication of occupational proactivity is the ability to fare relatively well even in a recessionary environment characterized by rapid labor market restructuring.

The preceding considerations allow for making some interesting insights on the nature of so-called information goods. When viewed through the lens of standard economic analysis, the very concept of information goods appears to be a contradiction in terms: as information is in principle infinitely replicable, it cannot be regarded as scarce, hence not being subject to the principle of economization. In other words, instead of being a genuine good, it should be seen as a general condition of action (Rothbard, 2004: 4). At first glance, this conclusion seems to be even further reinforced in the "information society", where, almost by definition, information becomes particularly abundant. This, however, would be a premature verdict.

As noted earlier, in a world saturated with endless torrents of data, in most cases, far from being general conditions of action, supposed pieces of valuable information are actually hindrances to action: instead of guiding agents to their intended goals, they are a source of cognitive disorientation and operational paralysis. By the same token, in such a world, genuinely valuable pieces of information, which require careful unearthing and judgmental processing, turn out to be paradigmatic examples of truly scarce goods, being neither naturally superabundant nor costlessly replicable. The former feature derives from their "hidden" nature, that is, from their being buried under an ever-shifting mass of "junk data", while the latter consists in the fact that the very difficulty of distinguishing between them and their cognitively useless counterparts implies that communicating their reliability to others (that is, replicating them successfully) is likely to be similarly difficult.

Thus, perhaps somewhat counterintuitively, obtaining and applying useful information in the "information society" necessitate creating and honing one's personal cognitive filters, which can be regarded as an essential component of one's unique structure of human capital. By extension, the same can be said of the individually processed data acquired with the use of such filters, which is thereby added to the structure in question: not as objective recipes, but as subjective, tacit competences and functional capabilities. This, again, indicates that information whose acquisition requires the deployment of proactive skills becomes necessarily individuated, hence revealing its nature as a scarce factor of production.

On this note, I would like to conclude my discussion of the major characteristics of the proactive society. As can be easily seen, they are as deep reaching as they are multidisciplinary. As, however, the present book is essentially a work of economic analysis, in the next chapter, I would like to raise the question of the extent to which reflecting on the characteristics under consideration promises to expand our understanding of the laws and principles of economics. Such an approach follows naturally from the methodological view that regards socioeconomic developments and transformations not as pretexts for questioning the logical structure of social cooperation but as springboards for investigating its hitherto unexplored ramifications (Wiśniewski, 2014: 45). Thus, rather than revolutionizing our insights into the nature of production, consumption, and distribution of goods, the advent of the proactive society offers an evolutionary enlargement of their accumulated treasure trove, similar to the intellectual expansions that took place with the onset of the industrial and the managerial society.

Let us then examine in more detail how far this enlargement may proceed.

Bibliography

Acemoglu, D., Restrepo, P., 2018. Artificial Intelligence, Automation and Work. NBER Working Paper No. 24196.

Ahmad, N., Seymour, R. G., 2008. Defining Entrepreneurial Activity: Definitions Supporting Frameworks for Data Collection. OECD Statistics Working Papers, 2008/01, OECD Publishing.

Arnold, D. G., Audi, R., Zwolinski, M., 2010. Recent work in ethical theory and its implications for business ethics. Business Ethics Quarterly 20 (4), 559–581.

Audretsch, D. B., 2009. The entrepreneurial society. The Journal of Technology Transfer 34 (3), 245–254.

Bawden, D., Robinson, L., 2021. Information Overload: An Overview. In: Redlawsk, D. P. (Ed.), Oxford Encyclopedia of Political Decision Making. Oxford University Press, Oxford.

Bear, A., Skorton, D., 2019. The world needs students with interdisciplinary education. Issues in Science and Technology 35 (2), 60–62.

Bjørnskov, C., Foss, N. J., 2008. Economic freedom and entrepreneurial activity: Some cross-country evidence. Public Choice 134 (3), 307–328.
Boettke, P. J., Coyne, C. J., Leeson, P., 2008. Institutional stickiness and the new development economics. American Journal of Economics and Sociology 67 (2), 331–358.
Boudreaux, D. J., Holcombe, R. G., 1989a. The Coasian and Knightian theories of the firm. Managerial and Decision Economics 10 (2), 147–154.
Boudreaux, D. J., Holcombe, R. G., 1989b. Government by contract. Public Finance Quarterly 17 (3), 264–280.
Brennan, L. L., 2011. The scientific management of information overload. Journal of Business and Management 17 (1), 121–134.
Campos Dias de Sousa, R. E., Howden, D., 2015. The efficient market conjecture. Quarterly Journal of Austrian Economics 18 (4), 378–408.
Caplan, B., 2011. The Myth of the Rational Voter. Princeton University Press.
Casey, G., 2012. Ethics and Economics: Friends or Foes? In: O'Rourke, F. (Ed.), Human Destinies: Philosophical Essays in Memory of Gerald Hanratty. University of Notre Dame Press, Notre Dame, IN.
Cho, V., Huang, X., 2012. Professional commitment, organizational commitment, and the intention to leave for professional advancement. Information Technology and People 25 (1), 31–54.
Coase, R. H., 1988. The Firm, the Market, and the Law. University of Chicago Press, Chicago, IL.
Coase, R. H., 1992. The institutional structure of production. American Economic Review 82 (4), 713–719.
Cséfalvay, Z., 2011. Searching for economic rationale behind gated communities: A public choice approach. Urban Studies 48 (4), 749–764.
De Jong, J., Wennekers, S., 2008. Intrapreneurship; Conceptualizing Entrepreneurial Employee Behavior. Research Report H200802, Zoetermeer: EIM.
Drumwright, M. E., Murphy, P. E., 2004. How advertising practitioners view ethics: Moral muteness, moral myopia, and moral imagination. Journal of Advertising 33 (2), 7–24.
Emmett, R. B., 2011. Frank H. Knight on the entrepreneur function in modern enterprise. Seattle University Law Review 34 (4), 1139–1154.
Engelhardt, L., 2013. Central planning's computation problem. Quarterly Journal of Austrian Economics 16 (2), 227–246.
Evans, A. J., Wenzel, N. G., 2013. A framework for the study of firms as constitutional orders. Constitutional Political Economy 24 (1), 2–18.
Foss, K., Foss, N. J., Klein, P. G., 2007. Original and derived judgment: An entrepreneurial theory of economic organization. Organization Studies 28 (12), 1893–1912.
Foss, K., Foss, N. J., Klein, P. G., Klein, S. K., 2007. The entrepreneurial organization of heterogeneous capital. Journal of Management Studies 44 (7), 1165–1186.
Foss, N. J., Klein, P. G., 2012. Organizing Entrepreneurial Judgment: A New Approach to the Firm. Cambridge University Press, Cambridge.
Foss, N. J., Klein, P. G., 2014. Why managers still matter. MIT Sloan Management Review 56 (1), 73–80.

Frese, M., Gielnik, M., 2014. The psychology of entrepreneurship. Annual Review of Organizational Psychology and Organizational Behavior 1, 413–438.

Fukuyama, F., 1996. Trust: The Social Virtues and the Creation of Prosperity. Simon and Schuster, New York.

Gaglio, C. M., 2004. The role of mental simulations and counterfactual thinking in the opportunity identification process. Entrepreneurship Theory and Practice 28 (6), 533–552.

Grant, A., Ashford, S., 2008. The dynamics of proactivity at work. Research in Organizational Behavior 28, 3–34.

Gwartney, J. D., Lawson, R. A., Holcombe, R. G., 1999. Economic freedom and the environment for economic growth. Journal of Institutional and Theoretical Economics (JITE)/Zeitschrift für die gesamte Staatswissenschaft 155 (4), 643–663.

Hall, B. H., Rosenberg, N. (Eds.), 2010. Handbook of the Economics of Innovation. North-Holland/Elsevier, Amsterdam, NL and Oxford, UK.

Hall, D. T., 2004. The protean career: A quarter-century journey. Journal of Vocational Behavior 65 (1), 1–13.

Hayek, F. A., 2002. Competition as a discovery procedure. Quarterly Journal of Austrian Economics 5 (3), 9–23.

Higgs, R., 1987. Crisis and Leviathan: Critical Episodes in the Growth of American Government. Oxford University Press, New York.

Higgs, R., 1997. Regime uncertainty: Why the great depression lasted so long and why prosperity resumed after the war. The Independent Review 1 (4), 561–590.

Holcombe, R. G., 2003. The origins of entrepreneurial opportunities. Review of Austrian Economics 16 (1), 25–43.

Hoppe, H.-H., 2007. The limits of numerical probability: Frank H. Knight and Ludwig von Mises and the frequency interpretation. Quarterly Journal of Austrian Economics 10 (1), 1–20.

Huemer, M., 2013. The Problem of Political Authority. Palgrave MacMillan, London.

Hülsmann, J. G., 1997. Political unification: A generalized progression theorem. Journal of Libertarian Studies 13 (1), 81–96.

Hülsmann, J. G., 2003. Facts and counterfactuals in economic law. Journal of Libertarian Studies 17 (1), 57–102.

Hülsmann, J. G., 2006. The political economy of moral hazard. Politická ekonomie 54 (1), 35–47.

Ikeda, S., 1997. Dynamics of the Mixed Economy: Toward a Theory of Interventionism. Routledge, New York.

Intan-Soraya, R., Chew, K. W., 2010. A framework for human resource management in the knowledge economy: Building intellectual capital and innovative capability. International Journal of Business and Management Science 3 (2), 251–273.

Kirzner, I. M., 1997. Entrepreneurial discovery and the competitive market process: An Austrian approach. Journal of Economic Literature 35 (1), 60–85.

Kirzner, I. M., 2009. The alert and creative entrepreneur: A clarification. Small Business Economics 32 (2), 145–152.
Kirzner, I. M., 2017. The entrepreneurial market process: An exposition. Southern Economic Journal 83 (4), 855–868.
Klein, P. G., 1996. Economic calculation and the limits of organization. Review of Austrian Economics 9 (2), 3–28.
Klein, P. G., 2008. Opportunity discovery, entrepreneurial action, and economic organization. Strategic Entrepreneurship Journal 2, 175–190.
Knight, F. H., 1985 [1921]. Risk, Uncertainty and Profit. University of Chicago Press, Chicago.
Koltko-Rivera, M. E., 2006. Rediscovering the later version of Maslow's hierarchy of needs: Self-transcendence and opportunities for theory, research, and unification. Review of General Psychology 10 (4), 302–317.
Langlois, R. N., 2003. The vanishing hand: The changing dynamics of industrial capitalism. Industrial and Corporate Change 12 (2), 351–385.
Langlois, R. N., 2007. The entrepreneurial theory of the firm and the theory of the entrepreneurial firm. Journal of Management Studies 44 (7), 1107–1124.
Lazear, E. P., 2004. Balanced skills and entrepreneurship. American Economic Review 94 (2), 208–211.
Lee, G., Elliott-Lee, D., 2006. Courage: The Backbone of Leadership. John Wiley & Sons.
Leeson, P. T., Coyne, C. J., 2012. Wisdom, alterability, and social rules. Managerial and Decision Economics 33 (5–6), 441–451.
Lerner, D. A., Hunt, R. A., Dimov, D., 2018. Action! Moving beyond the intendedly-rational logics of entrepreneurship. Journal of Business Venturing 33 (1), 52–69.
Lewin, P., Baetjer, H., 2011. The capital-based view of the firm. Review of Austrian Economics 24 (4), 335–354.
Long, R. T., 2006. Realism and abstraction in economics: Aristotle and Mises versus Friedman. Quarterly Journal of Austrian Economics 9 (3), 3–23.
Machan, T. R., 2009. The virtue of prudence as the moral basis of commerce. Reason Papers 31, 49–61.
Manish, G. P., Sutter, D., 2016. Mastery versus profit as motivation for the entrepreneur: How crony policies shape business. Journal of Entrepreneurship and Public Policy 5 (1), 95–112.
McAfee, R. P., McMillan, J., 1995. Organizational diseconomies of scale. Journal of Economics & Management Strategy 4 (3), 399–426.
McCaffrey, M., 2018. Extending the economic foundations of entrepreneurship research. European Management Review 14, 1–9.
McCaffrey, M., Salerno, J. T., 2011. A theory of political entrepreneurship. Modern Economy 2 (4), 552–560.
McCloskey, D., 2010. Bourgeois Dignity: Why Economics Can't Explain the Modern World. University of Chicago Press, Chicago, IL.
McCloskey, D., 2016. Bourgeois Equality: How Ideas, Not Capital or Institutions, Enriched the World. University of Chicago Press, Chicago, IL.
McMullen, J., 2015. Entrepreneurial judgment as empathic accuracy: A sequential decision-making approach to entrepreneurial action. Journal of Institutional Economics 11 (3), 651–681.

McMullen, J., Shepherd, D., 2006. Entrepreneurial action and the role of uncertainty in the theory of the entrepreneur. Academy of Management Review 31 (1), 132–152.

Mises, L., 2008 [1951]. Profit and Loss. Ludwig von Mises Institute, Auburn, AL.

Oguz, F., Sengun, A. E., 2011. Mystery of the unknown: Revisiting tacit knowledge in the organizational literature. Journal of Knowledge Management 15 (3), 445–461.

Olson, M., 1971 [1965]. The Logic of Collective Action: Public Goods and the Theory of Groups. Harvard University Press, Cambridge, MA.

Oppenheimer, F., 1922. The State. B.W. Huebsch, New York.

Packard, M. D., Clark, B. B., Klein, P. G., 2017. Uncertainty types and transitions in the entrepreneurial process. Organization Science 28 (5), 840–856.

Pellegrini, M. M., Ciappei, C., 2015. Ethical judgment and radical business changes: The role of entrepreneurial perspicacity. Journal of Business Ethics 128 (4), 769–788.

Porter, M. E., Kramer, M. R., 2006. Strategy and society: The link between competitive advantage and corporate social responsibility. Harvard Business Review 84 (12), 78–92.

Riordan, M. H., Williamson, O. E., 1985. Asset specificity and economic organization. International Journal of Industrial Organization 3 (4), 365–378.

Rothbard, M. N., 2004 [1962]. Man, Economy, and State, with Power and Market. Scholar's ed. Ludwig von Mises Institute, Auburn, AL.

Salerno, J. T., 2008. Imperialism and the logic of war making. The Independent Review 12 (3), 447–457.

Salerno, J. T., 2009. Lionel Robbins: Neoclassical maximizer or proto-praxeologist? Quarterly Journal of Austrian Economics 12 (4), 98–110.

Salerno, J. T., 2010. Menger's causal-realist analysis in modern economics. Review of Austrian Economics 23 (1), 1–16.

Sarasvathy, S. D., 2008. Effectuation: Elements of Entrepreneurial Expertise. Edward Elgar Publishing, Northampton, MA.

Somin, I., 2013. Democracy and Political Ignorance: Why Smaller Government Is Smarter. Stanford University Press, Redwood City, CA.

Standing, G., 2011. The Precariat. Bloomsbury Academic, London.

Steinbauer, R., Rhew, N., Kinnamon, E., Fabian, F., 2014. The conflicting drivers of entrepreneurial ethics. Journal of Ethics & Entrepreneurship 4 (1), 57–72.

Stewart, I., De, D., Cole, A., 2015. Technology and People: The Great Job-Creating Machine. Deloitte, London, UK.

Stockman, D., 2013. The Great Deformation: The Corruption of Capitalism in America. Public Affairs Press, New York.

Stringham, E., 2015. Private Governance: Creating Order in Economic and Social Life. Oxford University Press, New York.

Stringham, E. P., Hummel, J. R., 2010. If a pure market economy is so good, why doesn't it exist? The importance of changing preferences vs. incentives in social change. Quarterly Journal of Austrian Economics 13 (2), 31–52.

Taleb, N., 2012. Antifragile: Things That Gain from Disorder. Random House, New York.

von Hippel, E., Ogawa, S., de Jong, P. J., 2011. The age of consumer innovator. Sloan Management Review 53 (1), 27–35.

Wagner, R. E., 2014. Entangled political economy: A keynote address. Advances in Austrian Economics 16, 15–36.

Warren, R. C., 1994. Corporate temperance: A business virtue. Business Ethics: A European Review 3 (4), 223–232.

Webster, F., 2014. Theories of the Information Society. Routledge, London.

Werhane, P. H., 2002. Moral imagination and systems thinking. Journal of Business Ethics 38 (1), 33–42.

Williamson, O., 2000. The new institutional economics: Taking stock, looking ahead. Journal of Economic Literature 38 (3), 595–613.

Wiśniewski, J. B., 2014. The methodology of the Austrian school of economics: The present state of knowledge. Ekonomia – Wroclaw Economic Review 20 (1), 39–54.

Wiśniewski, J. B., 2019. Word, action, and entrepreneurship. Studies in Logic, Grammar and Rhetoric 57 (1), 161–174.

Wiśniewski, J. B., 2020. On the impossibility of intellectual property. Quarterly Journal of Austrian Economics 23 (1), 33–45.

Witt, U., 2007. Firms as realizations of entrepreneurial visions. Journal of Management Studies 44 (7), 1125–1140.

2 The proactive society and economic theory

2.1 Scarcity and value in the proactive society

Defining economics as the science of scarcity, while reasonable enough as a starting point, nonetheless runs the risk of postulating the state of "perfect satisfaction" as the ultimate endpoint of all human action. Even authors deeply steeped in the investigation of the dynamic market process sometimes regard such quietist abstractions as potentially useful analytical devices, if not as asymptotically achievable normative ideals (Packard, 2019). Hence the notion that the holy grail of general equilibrium is a viable benchmark against which the optimality of any given state of affairs can be assessed, even if one realizes that the concept in question is purely hypothetical and realistically unattainable.

Certain authors are willing to banish any musings about the extent to which a well-functioning economy can be expected to display the tendency toward long-run equilibrium, advising instead to focus on momentary states of rest that obtain as a result of successfully conducted voluntary transactions (Rothbard, 1995a). Even they, however, seem to be ultimately agnostic on the issue of whether endlessly imperturbable contentment that signifies the total elimination of scarcity can be considered as the final destination of economic growth and development.

What I would like to suggest here is that focusing one's attention on proactivity understood as an indispensable element of professional efficiency can shed new light on the subject at hand and substantiate the conclusion that, as far as purposive beings are concerned, "solving the problem of scarcity" is a contradiction in terms. As a proactive employee is expected not only to perform routine and predictable tasks handed down by higher-level management but also to apply himself spontaneously to qualitatively new challenges and be on the lookout for incoming opportunities, he should not regard completing his daily shift as tantamount to bringing his work environment closer to the state of final equilibrium. Rather, he should view his activity as continually actuating the system of large-scale social cooperation and expanding the range of manifestations of the phenomenon of human action.

DOI: 10.4324/9781003764557-3

Notice that this strictly processual understanding of economic progress helps avoid the problematic assumption that the optimal situation for a purposive being is to turn into a vegetative being. At the same time, however, it does not impugn the value of analytical devices such as Pareto-superiority, "plain states of rest", and "momentary equilibria" (Salerno, 2006: 45–46), which allow for distinguishing between economically better and worse outcomes.

As the concept of the proactive society emphasizes the broadly conceived entrepreneurial character of all human action, the open-ended character of proactive employee orientation can be easily extrapolated to full-blooded entrepreneurial functions as well. Surprisingly enough, even here, all mention of entrepreneurial dynamism and innovativeness notwithstanding, the main goal of economic activity is often conceptualized as equilibration, which can be criticized as unrealistic and operationally meaningless (Foss and Klein, 2010). More curiously still, even Schumpeterian entrepreneurs, who constitute the driving force behind "creative destruction", are often ultimately seen as setting the parameters of new equilibrium states waiting to be achieved by their Kirznerian counterparts. However, when analyzing an environment in which proactivity is a universally desirable personal trait, one can easily reject the notion that everlasting quietude is the ne plus ultra of economic success or even the ideal, if only hypothetical benchmark of Pareto-optimality.

When seen from this point of view, resourcefully confronting unforeseen contingencies, continuously addressing novel conundrums, and perceptively exploiting ever-shifting opportunities can be regarded as possessing intrinsic rather than just instrumental value (Joo and Lim, 2009). This, in turn, reinforces the conclusion that the satisfaction of purposeful agents is derived not just from the attainment of their goals but from the maintenance of their preparedness for and effectiveness in achieving those goals as well. The latter, however, is logically incompatible with settling into any final state of rest. In other words, the proactive approach to welfare improvement is focused not only on outcomes but on dispositions and capabilities as well.

In response, one might object by suggesting that putting things this way makes the concept of economic growth and development hopelessly unintelligible. After all, if being closer to or further away from the hypothetical state of final equilibrium cannot be treated as a meaningful yardstick in this context, how else is one to evaluate the relative prosperity or lack thereof of any given economy?

The most straightforward answer to this objection is the blunt assertion that, in view of the impossibility of making scientifically valid interpersonal comparisons of utility, economic growth and development are ultimately somewhat fuzzy, psychologically contingent, and culture-specific concepts. In other words, stagnant agricultural societies can be justifiably regarded as underdeveloped as compared with their dynamic service-based counterparts, only given the psychologically and anthropologically reasonable assumption that broadly conceived material well-being occupies a universally prominent position in the scale of human values. To push the matter further and demand more objective criteria of social welfare would be to fall prey to the kind of physicalism or ethicism that is wholly irreconcilable with the fundamental insights of the marginalist revolution (Wiśniewski, 2020a).

This is not to say, however, that the presence of phenomena such as specialization, division of labor, capital accumulation, introduction of innovations, trade integration, and entrepreneurialism cannot be said to make a given economy better off when judged by the proactive standard. The crucial distinction here is that instead of suggesting that such phenomena bring the economy closer to the state of final equilibrium, the proactive approach proposes that they enhance social welfare insofar as they expand the scale and scope of human action, allowing for an ever-greater realization of its cooperative potential.

This approach is quantitatively tangible in a way that makes it largely compatible with the application of standard macroeconomic indicators such as GDP, which can be treated as a fairly reliable proxy for the breadth and depth of social cooperation taking place in a given territory. On the other hand, it is also sufficiently steeped in qualitative considerations to account for the fact that such indicators are trustworthy only if the cooperation they aim to reflect is embedded in a genuinely internalized framework of cultural norms, informal institutions, and behavioral dispositions (Coyne and Boettke, 2006). In sum, the perspective in question by no means denies the intelligibility of concepts such as economic growth and development, but it emphasizes that these are not purely instrumentally valuable processes whose final destination is blissful stagnation.

That being said, consistent application of the proactive orientation brings into the foreground the fact that a sufficiently open-ended understanding of economic growth and development can generate a divergence between their purely quantitative indicators and the corresponding qualitative preconditions. For instance, having reached a certain threshold of material well-being brought about by the processes of urbanization, a considerable segment of a given society may decide to move to the countryside to enjoy higher levels of bonding capital (Sørensen, 2016), even at the expense of abandoning the majority of typically urban amenities and prospects for career advancement. Likewise, having enriched itself by means of globalization and the attendant ability to exploit the worldwide benefits of absolute and comparative advantage, a certain portion of a given society may desist from patronizing global corporations in favor of small-scale local companies, seeing the products of the latter as more culturally attractive and intimately trustworthy (Prigent-Simonin and Hérault-Fournier, 2005), even if more expensive.

It should be noted that examples such as the ones mentioned above need not be construed as manifestations of voluntarily accepted "degrowth" or "de-development", but rather as proactive efforts to modify one's consumer choices (and thus the shape of the market that aims to satisfy them) in accordance with one's changing preference scale, which, in this instance, becomes more attuned to strictly qualitative and culturally embedded considerations. As such considerations are by definition excluded from GDP and similar indicators, such value reorientations may create a false impression that the individuals involved have opted for a self-inflicted retrogression. However, the only way to avoid mistaking such an impression for reality is not to construct more "inclusive" equivalents of GDP, but to realize that scarcity is a moving target and that, as material needs become increasingly satisfied, the means and ends subject to economization may become increasingly intangible as judged by an external observer.

In fact, if the qualitative demands and cultural considerations described above become sufficiently widespread in a given society and if their incorporation into specific goods and services becomes a sine qua non of their market desirability, then the "measurement problem" sketched in the preceding paragraph essentially solves itself. This is because under such circumstances, goods that do not meet the above requirements lose their goods-character, thus being excluded from the GDP and other indicators that aspire to numerical precision. Consequently, the standard approach to quantifying economic growth and development can be applied even in the proactive world, provided that the value commitments of its inhabitants are sufficiently prevalent and well internalized.

However, the suggested solution to this macro-issue in no way diminishes the difficulty of the underlying entrepreneurial challenge of satisfying a normatively fastidious customer base. It might be argued that the proactive society is characterized by a particularly pronounced degree of consumer activism (Hilton, 2009), whereby consumers routinely innovate and refine their tastes in a quasi-Schumpeterian manner. And yet, they need not be thought of as necessarily eager to translate these tastes into well-defined preferences and demands for highly specified goods, as doing so would require them to assume the full-blooded entrepreneurial role or engage in self-sufficient production instead of remaining in the position of customers awaiting satisfaction. In other words, unless we imagine the proactive society to be an environment populated exclusively by full-scale entrepreneurs – which is a logical impossibility bound to short-circuit the market system of specialized cooperation and coordinated teamwork – we must assume a certain degree of passive receptivity on the part of even highly purpose-driven consumers.

This means that entrepreneurs willing to please proactively oriented customers can neither simply manufacture wants through motivational advertising and impose them on their client base, nor can they simply discover or forecast any well-defined preferences of their clients and tap into them. Instead, they need to discover or forecast the more or less amorphous preferences of their customers and integrate them into innovative narratives capable of attracting the attention of qualitatively demanding individuals (Roundy, 2021). That is to say, in the environment under consideration, economic value is neither purely created nor purely discovered by entrepreneurs, but is rather cocreated and co-discovered by entrepreneurs and their customers, with the former retaining the ultimately "active" role.

The emergence of this kind of relationship allows for deploying a range of novel business strategies that may provide illuminating illustrations capable of expanding our understanding of the nuances of value theory. For instance, offering high-priced goods that embody charitable concerns, ethical aspirations, or cultural identities might fit well into the atmosphere of Veblen-style conspicuous consumption, with the crucial caveat that the conspicuity in question refers not to material extravagance, but to normative fastidiousness (Johnson, Tariq, and Baker, 2018). In such cases, higher prices may go hand in hand with higher demand insofar as consumers exhibit a pronounced demand for social status understood in axiological terms, even if such status does not perform any external signaling function.

Likewise, operating in a proactive society allows for appreciating certain hitherto scantily explored aspects of the law of imputation. Just as the value of final goods is imputed backwards to the capital goods used to produce the former, the value delivered to one's direct beneficiaries can sometimes be imputed backwards to their indirect counterparts. Such situations appear particularly likely to occur in connection with endeavors that fall within the ambit of so-called social entrepreneurship (Brooks, 2008). In contrast to typical charitable organizations, "social enterprises" are expected to sustain themselves not on the basis of fundraising and donations, but by standard business methods of providing goods and services sold at a profit, the only difference being that the generated profits are to be devoted to maximizing "social impact". If, however, the term "social impact" is to be substantially differentiated from the more mundane notion of "consumer satisfaction", the former inevitably acquires connotations of unprofitability. This, in turn, might seem to make the whole idea of social entrepreneurship internally contradictory and self-defeating.

Consumer proactivity, however, could endow this idea with unprecedented economic viability. More specifically, if a considerable part of the consuming public were to place a special premium on the satisfaction derived from contributing to charitable efforts, then a mature market of social enterprises could address its wants in a commercially professional and meticulously tailored manner. One can easily imagine that under such circumstances, the ability of social entrepreneurs to solve the plight of their direct beneficiaries would be rewarded proportionally by their indirect beneficiaries, that is, their paying customers understood not so much as classical donors, but rather as regular buyers of philanthropic gratification. Consequently, achieving social impact could become in principle no less profitable than more narrowly defined commercial objectives. Fully businesslike economic calculation could then be applied to the activities of social enterprises, even if, by definition, it would have to continue operating in a roundabout, imputed fashion (Wiśniewski, 2022: 6–7).

Finally, establishing a solid base of proactively oriented customers highlights a perhaps underappreciated aspect of the network effect. As conscious and entrepreneurially minded consumers can be expected not only to offer constructive feedback but also to engage in innovative tinkering with purchased products (Desouza et al., 2008), they can be regarded as genuinely contributive to the productivity of their favorite businesses. Thus, in a proactive environment, reaching as great a number of users as possible with one's goods and services can result in the emergence of not only a network of dedicated enthusiasts who drive the adoption of certain standards but also a network of spontaneous researchers who drive the improvement of these standards.

In other words, proactively driven network effects can generate the kind of "prosumption" that assumes neither the form of commons-based peer activities, nor that of the commercial "sharing economy": that is, the kind that is neither nonprofit nor for-profit based on the independent contractor model, but for-profit in a robustly entrepreneurial sense. More specifically, it can create prosumers who are neither merely hobbyist inventors, nor simply consumers who convert their durable assets into factors of production according to already existing entrepreneurial schemes, but authentic innovators capable of generating monetizable externalities for the companies patronized by them. It is then up to individual companies to decide whether to help internalize such externalities by rewarding their originators, thereby hopefully promoting prosumer innovativeness, or whether to leave them monetarily uncompensated out of fear of destroying their spirit of spontaneous and gratuitous creativity.

In conclusion, theoretical reflection on the nature of the proactive society allows for extending the legacy of the marginalist-subjectivist revolution in economics in the direction of more consistently qualitative treatment of the subjects of scarcity and value. These, in turn, can both inform and be informed by the emergence of novel business practices aimed at satisfying a consumer public that is increasingly quasi-entrepreneurial in the sense of continuously refining its tastes and improving its feedback. However, determining the more precise character of the opportunities and challenges attending the implementation of such practices requires investigating the ways in which the concept of widespread proactivity can illuminate the theory of capital and production. Let us then turn to these issues now.

2.2 Capital and production in the proactive society

If we accept the definition of entrepreneurship as the exercise of business judgment with respect to one's own capital structure of production (Foss and Klein, 2012), we should naturally embrace the conclusion that in the proactive society, not only high-level managers but also rank-and-file employees, consumers, and other non-owners of corporate assets are likely to influence processes of production in an increasingly autonomous way.

This realization has important implications for a variety of aspects and stages that comprise productive activities. First, it is a well-established truth that production is the opportunity cost of consumption, which implies that initiating productive processes requires deferring gratification and accumulating savings that constitute the so-called subsistence fund (Braun and Howden, 2017). Likewise, it is well known that in a mature economic system grounded in the division of labor, a budding entrepreneur can rely on a broad range of external financing sources, including bank loans, private equity capital, and public equity issuance. A less appreciated fact, on the other hand, is that in the proactive society, one can dispense with the financial resources and transactional intermediation of professional institutions and raise capital directly from one's current and prospective customers.

In other words, while the managerial society is based on a relatively pronounced functional distinction between entrepreneurs who seek growth capital and capitalists who provide it (Klein, 2010), in its proactive counterpart, such functional distinctions become increasingly blurred, so much so that under such conditions, "nonprofessional" consumer-investors may become the most attractive group of external financiers. Unsurprisingly, this is due to the fact that such individuals, as end users, are particularly concerned about the quality of the goods they receive, and thus, as investors, they are likely to be particularly sensitive to the entrepreneurial potential of the firms they decide to support.

Moreover, this concern and sensitivity are bound to be enhanced even further if we take into account the prosumer orientation of proactive clients, which, in this context, allows them to become not just investors but also indirect activist investors in the companies they patronize. That is to say, even if, due to the dispersion of their ownership stakes, they are unlikely to influence the decisions of executive directors and supervisory boards as residual claimants, their potential creative input into the character of goods and services offered on the market can, in practical terms, allow them to co-direct the strategic development of corporate business plans.

Next, it should be noted that insofar as the transition to the proactive society is a result of crossing a critical threshold of technological progress, productive specialization, professional mobility, and similar wealth-enhancing developments, the disposable income of its average member is likely to exhibit substantial growth. This, other things being equal, should lead to an unprecedented saturation of the loan market with private savings, thereby driving down interest rates and making low-risk investment vehicles increasingly unattractive (Hülsmann, 2016: 86). This, in turn, should provide further encouragement to consumer-investors to buy shares in more speculative enterprises, whose value propositions they can proactively co-create, especially at an early stage of their development.

In addition to the nature of business financing, widespread proactivity is bound to impact the internal dynamic of commercial production as well. From the point of view of the owner-entrepreneur, implementing a business model can follow the causal or the effectual approach, the latter being particularly useful in an environment of exceptionally heightened uncertainty, including that related to the productive capabilities of the resources at one's disposal. If, however, some of the human resources under one's supervision are expected to exhibit proactive behavior, then the business model of one's firm should evolve based not just on entrepreneurial effectuation but also on its intrapreneurial counterpart (Brenk, Lüttgens, Diener, and Piller, 2019). In other words, in the proactive society, corporate goals should be recalibrated not only because owner-entrepreneurs learn more about the subjectively useful attributes of their assets, but also because their employees learn more about the productive potential of their tacit knowledge, teamwork synergies, spontaneous problem-solving skills, etc.

As the supply of human capital consists of persons, not objects, the process whereby its economic value manifests itself is one not simply of discovery, but of self-discovery. Thus, the role of the company owner in fostering intrapreneurial effectuation consists not in micromanagement, but in creating an institutional environment for fruitful self-management within well-specified limits. That is to say, the primary function of the owner-entrepreneur in the processes of production taking place in the proactive society is to harness the constructive power of an open-ended economic universe (Cordato, 2013) while making sure that the open-endedness in question is organizationally disciplined and subject to sound macro-scale strategic direction.

This task is beset with a number of challenges unique to the domain of human capital management, especially when continuous proactivity on the part of the managed individuals is involved. For instance, when an entrepreneur wishes to avoid a potential holdup problem by gaining a permanent control over production-specific assets, he might resort to vertical integration, but the same solution is not viable in the context of human assets. This is because purposive individuals, unlike non-human resources, retain free will even under the conditions of the employment relation and the corresponding contractual obligations. This, in turn, makes them inherently susceptible to the moral hazard of withholding their production-specific skills, which might result in derailing the operational efficiency of their employer's business. Needless to say, this internal form of the holdup problem becomes particularly acute when applied to individuals who, in virtue of their proactive status, are expected to act in a self-starting manner and use discretionary control over the resources entrusted to their care.

One potential answer to the above predicament is to rely not so much on the vertical integration of the production chain, but on the intra-firm integration of human, social, and institutional capital (Leitch, McMullan, and Harrison, 2013). More specifically, a successful entrepreneur operating in a proactive environment should be able to embed the human capital of his employees in a broader network of disciplining inter-employee relationships and a formal structure of corporate governance that sustains and enhances them. Thus, an employee willing to withhold his production-specific skills for reasons of opportunism or negligence should be reprimanded by his coworkers and softly pressured by them into contractually promised compliance. Likewise, he should be immediately flagged by a well-functioning system of formal incentives as ineligible for promotion, pay raise, and other performance-based rewards or as eligible for demotion, pay decrease, and other performance-based penalties.

The above example highlights the fact that capital complementarity pertains not only to capital goods within a given structure of production and to capital structures within the overall economy but to distinct categories of capital as well. In other words, it suggests that far from being a narrowly technical challenge or an exclusively commercial undertaking, successful capital management requires applied systems thinking, that is, the ability to foster the development of qualitatively differentiated and emergently dynamic combinatorial wholes (Harper and Endres, 2010). Furthermore, it should be noted in this connection that thinking in terms of a system implies the ability to integrate the internal framework of one's firm with the external structure of social and cultural norms: in the case under consideration, the formal and informal penalties of the corporate incentive system and the broader ethos of ostracizing those whose professional history is riddled with examples of incompetence and undependability.

It might also be added here that an entrepreneur who is proactive even by the standards of his profession may engage in educational and promotional efforts aimed at influencing the external culture in the appropriate direction: in this case, the direction of ruthlessly tracking down and exposing individuals with a bad track record of on-the-job reliability. This kind of "cultural entrepreneurship" (Klamer, 2011) can allow him to shape not only the planned order of his company's framework but also, albeit to a significantly smaller degree, the spontaneous order of the surrounding normative environment. In other words, it turns out that in the proactive society, leveraging the complementarity between different categories of capital may require adopting a premeditated and calculative approach even to those phenomena that are typically regarded as textbook examples of unplanned arrangements.

One significant example of the above task is the necessity of maintaining appropriate value commitments in the intergenerational perspective so that a proactive society does not slip back into a reactive mindset. In this connection, it might be argued that individuals who inhabit a wealthy society and live off the dividends and capital gains whose steady accrual they owe to previous generations are under particular risk of engaging in accelerated capital consumption or recklessly speculative investments. Hence, they are increasingly likely to take their wealth for granted and lose the proactivity – including its prudential and abstinential aspects – that is indispensable for preserving the productivity of their economy. This, in turn, suggests that one crucial role of entrepreneurs and other dedicated cultural activists in such an environment is to maintain and reinforce the society-wide "ethical structure of production" (Wiśniewski, 2022).

In other words, an essential task of such groups is to ensure the compatibility between the existing pool of physical and institutional capital on the one hand and the normative attitudes and cultural habits of its beneficiaries on the other. And while it would be unreasonable to opine from the armchair on the most promising method of meeting this goal, it is plausible to single out the encouragement of prosumer culture as perhaps the most natural blueprint for the development of more detailed strategies in this area. After all, cultivating the luxury of conscious consumption and the attendant opportunity for innovative tinkering may well be the most obvious way of bridging the gap between economic well-being and continued developmental ambition.

Another noteworthy instance of combining the planned order of one's business operations with the spontaneous order of the surrounding cultural milieu is the activation of "dead capital" (de Soto, 2000) by means of creating special economic zones and other pockets of alternative institutional arrangements. Such endeavors may be justifiably defined as manifestations of higher-order proactivity: that is, proactivity whose primary goal is to unleash the latent proactivity of others. The crucial point to keep in mind here is that the relevant entrepreneurial task is not so much to teach one's prospective employees how to adopt a self-starting and forward-looking attitude, but to attract those local individuals who already possess the appropriate characteristics while being unable to utilize them due to a stifling institutional climate. That is to say, the "higher-order" challenge in question consists in creating constitutional frameworks that allow for the spontaneous flourishing of the hitherto dormant human capital, which, in turn, may spur increasingly ambitious acts of institutional entrepreneurship down the road.

It is worth noting here that in a genuinely globalized world, combining the capital resources of planned and spontaneous orders may be supplemented by synthesizing the organizational potential of individual institutional designs, even if the latter are separated by vast physical distances. More specifically, useful bonding capital can be generated by means of "diplomatic entrepreneurship" (Acuto, 2013) driven by owners of special economic zones, charter cities, and other truly contractual governance structures. Such entrepreneurship, centered around sharing knowledge pertaining to the activation of "dead capital", the effective use of the exit option, and other methods of unlocking stifled employee productivity, can be said to embody a two-tiered approach to the promotion of proactivity, bringing together both its frontline practitioners and its institutional enablers. This kind of knowledge interchange can be seen as particularly fruitful insofar as the proactive society naturally aids the transition from hired workers to full-blooded entrepreneurs: consequently, those employees whose human capital was actuated within tailor-made organizational frameworks may be singularly suited to eventually become successful institutional entrepreneurs in their own right.

Finally, the present section should not be concluded without suggesting how the advent of widespread proactivity may influence one's understanding of the economic nature of capitalism, especially if one defines the system in question in terms of its unique ability to accelerate the accumulation of capital goods and appraise them with quantitative precision by means of monetary capital (Braun, 2017).

It goes without saying that the distributional features of capitalism have long been criticized on class-based grounds for their connection with the allegedly inherently exploitative nature of interest and profit. It is also well known that such critiques have been extensively rebutted by reputable theorists of the market process. Most notably in this regard, it was pointed out that interest is remuneration for advancing present funds to factors of production (Böhm-Bawerk, 1949), while profit is the reward for successful uncertainty bearing (Knight, 1985), with the crucial qualification that actual businesspeople typically perform both of these functions and earn incomes that inextricably combine both of the corresponding reward components (Salerno, 2008).

Reflecting on the essence of entrepreneurship in the proactive society can supplement such rebuttals with additional arguments. First, it might be noted that next to pure interest income and profits associated with successful business forecasts, entrepreneurs can generate earnings in the forms of decision-making rents, that is, returns to "the ultimate technical, supervisory, and organizational decisions that a capitalist-entrepreneur alone must make with respect to the disposition of his productive property" (Salerno, 2018: 198). While the concept in question may initially seem somewhat abstruse, it becomes more concrete when grounded in the differential advantage possessed by entrepreneurs particularly capable of exercising higher-order proactivity, that is, the ability to attract self-starting employees, encourage proxy-entrepreneurship among them and reduce the attendant moral hazard, leverage their teamwork synergies, etc.

As such special ownership rents are unique to the individual who displays competent control over his business assets, it makes no logical sense to describe them as economically exploitative. Furthermore, as each such individual constitutes a separate, one-person class, it makes little sense to account for the profitability of his activities in class-based terms. In sum, in the proactive society, the uniqueness of the entrepreneurial function and its productive contribution to economic output stands out with particular clarity, which renders the assertion of the supposedly intrinsically parasitic character of interest and profit conspicuously unconvincing.

Second, as proactivity is intimately associated with social mobility, its widespread presence is thoroughly incompatible with a rigid class-based vision of society and the economy. A number of pertinent phenomena can be mentioned here, including the advent of proxy-entrepreneurship, the increasing likelihood of transitioning from a hired worker to a full-scale firm owner, and the emergence of prosumers who assume the role of well-informed activist investors. All such developments point to the progressively blurred distinction between "the working class" and "the business class" under proactive capitalism and suggest that insofar as the currently dominant socioeconomic system involves their institutional repression, it is not capitalism, but its deformed caricature (Stockman, 2013).

Finally, next to the exploitation theory of profit and interest, it is the labor theory of value that constitutes the cornerstone of the traditional class-based critique of capitalism. However, in the proactive society, where labor in the most tangible, physical sense is increasingly performed by machines, which are by definition unexploitable in the socioeconomic meaning of the term, the labor theory of value turns out to be exceptionally incapable of accounting for the logical relationship between wages and productivity. After all, in such a society, the productivity of hired workers and the initiative of regular customers are increasingly rewarded not with wages and discounts, but with quasi-profits associated with assuming the role of proxy-entrepreneurs and quasi-interest associated with assuming the role of prosumer-capitalists. This demonstrates, perhaps more strikingly than any other hitherto known set of economic arrangements, that the ultimate source of market value consists not in material toil, but in utility-driven intentionality.

In conclusion, analyzing the theory of capital and production through the lens of the proactive society offers actionable insights into the nature of phenomena such as worker empowerment, intra-firm mobility, and consumer crowdfunding. At the same time, however, it emphasizes the indispensable function of firm owners and top-level executives in creating and maintaining cooperative frameworks that both promote and discipline such forms of proactivity.

The foregoing remarks may be taken to suggest that, insofar as the social model described here taps into the resourcefulness of individuals typically regarded as docile and reactive, it fosters an economy that is far more competitive than the one currently prevailing in the capitalist world. Whether this is the case, however, and whether reflecting on the nature of the proactive society can expand our understanding of competition will be the focus of the next section.

2.3 Monopoly and competition in the proactive society

Even though monopoly is a concept that can be defined in a number of ways, none of the relevant definitions describe it as a desirable state of affairs. Most characterizations suggest that monopolies reduce social welfare in virtue of hampering the competitive pressure that reduces prices and increases quality. Some, on the other hand, view them as a natural and harmless market phenomenon. Thus, a given socioeconomic system can be regarded as being conducive to efficiency inasmuch as it can be demonstrated to prevent the emergence of "bad" monopolies and prove the harmlessness of the remaining ones. In what follows, I shall attempt to argue that the proactive society can be justifiably seen as meeting these criteria.

Among the conditions of so-called perfect competition propounded by the neoclassical monopoly theory, there are requirements such as many buyers and sellers, perfect information, and perfect factor mobility. With respect to the first of these, the proactive society can be expected to enjoy a particularly abundant proliferation of separate business entities. As pointed out in Chapter 1, Section 1.3, this is due to a number of factors, including: (1) the emergence of widespread proxy-entrepreneurship and the attendant heightened willingness to join the ranks of firm owners, (2) the necessity of attracting specialized intellectual capital coupled with the operationally crippling danger of "monopolizing" the micro-markets in which it is traded, (3) the reduced need for vertical integration in a technologically advanced and logistically efficient environment, and (4) the requirement of building corporate governance structures that are "institutionally sticky" and thus typically rather small in size to ensure sufficient social intimacy.

With regard to the condition of perfect information, the proactive society can be said to approximate it insofar as its members can be expected to display cognitive resourcefulness and intellectual initiative. More specifically, as indicated in Chapter 1, Section 1.6: 1) the human-centeredness of genuinely proactive employees necessitates that they approach informational challenges in a robustly qualitative (i.e., prudently selective) manner, 2) the promotion of proxy-entrepreneurship demands the establishment of organizational frameworks conducive to the elicitation of tacit employee knowledge, and 3) the advent of protean careers goes hand in hand with heightened responsiveness to changing market data exhibited by individuals in possession of specific cognitive capabilities.

Finally, as far as factor mobility is concerned, one should note in particular the eagerness of proactive career builders to look for the kinds of institutional frameworks in which their unique human capital can flourish. That is to say, as suggested in Chapter 1, Section 1.4, that such individuals are especially likely to make sound strategic use of voice and exit options, meaning that they are not hesitant to leave or secede from what they regard as politically stifling environments and subsequently establish communities of like-minded persons where their respective productive potentials can be actualized more fully.

That being said, there are certain important respects in which the proactive society deviates from the formal ideal of perfect competition. First, the flourishing of entrepreneurship, both in its full-blooded and proxy variety, together with the emergence of widespread prosumer innovativeness, is more likely than not to result in a significantly increased product heterogeneity.

Second, the proactive society is a fertile field for the continuous emergence of novel organizational forms, previously unheard-of industries, and other qualitatively new additions to the existing configuration of market data, which might result in a constantly elevated level of transaction costs. And even if it is fair to assume that reducing transaction costs is an important facet of strategic firm-level proactivity, the countervailing forces of exogenous transactional dynamism might generate a tug-of-war situation in which the traditional Coasian task of the firm becomes enduringly more complex than it is in the more predictable and routinized environment of the managerial society.

Finally, as noted in the previous section of the present chapter, proactively oriented enterprises can flourish by making an extensive use of network effects, especially those associated with the advent of prosumer-innovators. This, in turn, can be expected to create significant positive externalities whose internalization might be inadvisable for fear of stifling their spontaneous productivity.

Hence, all in all, as there is no objective method of evaluating the respective weight of the constitutive conditions of perfect competition, it ultimately appears impossible to determine whether the proactive society is more likely to approach this model than its more reactive counterparts are. However, as even its alleged shortcomings vis-à-vis the model in question seem clearly conducive to economic development and consumer welfare, there is all the more reason to discard perfect competition as a viable ideal of efficiency (Hayek, 1948) instead of faulting the proactive society for not approximating all of its requirements.

By the same token, one might suggest that reflecting on the nature of the proactive society furnishes additional arguments against identifying monopolists with single sellers of specific goods or services. This is primarily due to the fact that in a world that places a high premium on a self-starting and forward-looking attitude, broadly conceived entrepreneurialism is promoted among all groups of market participants, and the common denominator of all varieties of entrepreneurialism is the introduction of qualitatively new data (i.e., data unique to a given seller) into the realm of social cooperation.

In this sense, Schumpeterian innovators become "monopolists" in virtue of supplying novel offerings, Kirznerian arbitrageurs become "monopolists" in virtue of identifying novel profit opportunities (including those in the form of simple price spreads between hitherto insufficiently examined markets), and Knightian uncertainty-bearers become "monopolists" in virtue of making unique insights into future constellations of market data. The bottom line here is that in order to qualify as an entrepreneur, one needs to be able to profit by means of "selling" one's singular take on economic reality, which is the ultimate factor of production responsible for determining the productivity of various combinations of the traditional three factors (Erken, Donselaar, and Thurik, 2018).

The above observation is bolstered even further by the realization that in a proactive society, the necessity of acquiring quasi-entrepreneurial competences is extended to non-company owners as well. Thus, even lower-level employees may be regarded as "monopolists" in view of being the sole sellers of their individual methods of dealing with unique client problems, singular frontline contingencies, personal career changes, etc. This follows inevitably from the consistently subjectivist recognition of the fact that economic value resides neither in the physical nor in the intellectual attributes of a given good, but in its purposive deployment in an environment of scarcity and uncertainty aimed at fulfilling hitherto unsatisfied wants (Wiśniewski, 2020a).

It might also be noted in this context that in the proactive society, the vast majority of market participants – firms and individuals alike – engage in product differentiation in virtue of striving continually to prove their unique edge in dealing with idiosyncratic market events. This, however, far from generating monopolistic deadweight losses, drives economic progress by introducing innovations and spurring companies to keep outdoing one another in terms of innovativeness (Holcombe, 2009). Unsurprisingly, this indicates that the economic benefits of the proactive society cannot be captured in a static neoclassical framework, but such a conclusion appears to impugn the usefulness of the latter rather than the welfare potential of the former.

Next, in this connection, it should be emphasized once again that the proactive society is likely to exhibit a pronounced degree of intertemporal variability on account of factors such as prosumer initiative, career mobility, and unhampered institutional experimentation. This, needless to say, greatly amplifies the difficulty of piercing the veil of uncertainty and magnifies the challenge of navigating the temporal dimension of entrepreneurial operations (Garrison, 2001). Hence, entrepreneurs who conduct their businesses under such circumstances cannot be faulted for exploiting various strategies aimed at earning "extraordinary" profits treated as protective buffers against unpredictable contingencies (Hoppe, 2009).

To take a specific example, an entrepreneur in the apple industry might decide to exploit what he regards as a temporary inelasticity of demand for his products in order to earn the extra revenue needed to transition to the orange industry. This, however, should not be construed as the earning of a monopoly rent, but rather as a textbook example of exercising entrepreneurial judgment. One should notice that there are at least two major aspects involved with respect to which the businessman in question can be mistaken: that of whether his customers will in fact bear paying temporarily higher prices and that of whether in the longer run oranges will actually become more desirable foodstuffs than apples. Thus, far from reaping unfair monopoly profits, in taking the course of action under consideration, he exposes himself to potential losses.

Furthermore, as the "monopolistic" and the "entrepreneurial" interpretation of the relevant price increases may be equally consistent with the visible behavioral data at hand, opting for the former and subsequently hurling accusations of anticompetitive practices might be justifiably seen as analytically groundless. After all, the intentions behind specific business decisions and the corresponding evaluations of their profitability are ultimately accessible exclusively to the entrepreneur involved and assessable solely in terms of counterfactual scenarios, which are necessarily unseen to external observers (Hülsmann, 2003).

This suggests that the only economically meaningful criterion for determining whether the pursuit of a given business strategy is competitive or monopolistic (in the sense of being Pareto-superior or Pareto-inferior) is neither the number of entities in a given industry nor the elasticity of demand for their products, but the presence or absence of legal barriers to entry and the corresponding political privileges or lack thereof (Block, 2008). This, in turn, implies that a society that is undergoing the transition from the managerial phase to the proactive phase is likely to be particularly harmed by the erection of such barriers and the establishment of such privileges.

Several main factors merit mentioning here. First, accelerated automation of routine tasks reorients human productivity in the direction of "higher-order", irreducibly human skills of harnessing the potential of automated processes in the service of increasingly differentiated consumer wants. Shielding politically connected firms from the dynamic of the market process by granting them monopolistic favors creates a major impediment to this reorientation, as it artificially conserves obsolete modes of business operation and prevents the formation of the requisite human capital. In this sense, the establishment of legally protected monopolies generates islands of capital miscalculation similar to the ones that arise in the course of implementing all kinds of centrally planned industrial policies (Glavan, Anghel, and Avrigeanu, 2010).

Under such conditions, technological development can become seriously misaligned with the development of the personal and interpersonal competencies needed for the creative and problem-specific use of novel technological solutions, resulting in a potentially adversarial relationship between the two. In other words, in such circumstances, technological capital and human capital can become substitutes rather than complements, which, in turn, may lead to protracted technological unemployment in those cases where a legal monopoly lays off its long-time employees.

Second, politically enforced monopolies stunt the flourishing of proxy-entrepreneurship. This is primarily due to the fact that as such institutions are artificially insulated from the market test of profit and loss, the same is eo ipso true of their employees who would otherwise have to exercise genuine business judgment in their dealings with customers and other relevant actors. Worse still, just like their ultimate bosses, the employees in question might be encouraged under such conditions to be particularly proactive in the domain of rent-seeking – that is, they might engage in "political proxy-entrepreneurship" or "non-productive intrapreneurship" (Elert and Stenkula, 2022).

In addition, the existence of legal barriers to entry hinders the transition of exceptionally proactive proxy-entrepreneurs into the ranks of full-blooded firm owners, thus preventing them from actualizing the fullness of their productive potential. Alternatively, the potential under discussion might be misdirected and ultimately wasted if such individuals manage to jump over all the relevant hurdles in virtue of becoming full-scale "political entrepreneurs" – that is, those who are singularly adept at maintaining the fossilized status quo instead of tearing down its walls.

Finally, if the number of business entities present in the market is artificially restricted on account of some of them possessing monopoly privileges, it might become particularly difficult to engage in the effectual process of self-discovery whereby pursuing a protean career allows one to form a clear, experiential vision of one's unique structure of human capital. In other words, if the number of available qualitatively distinct workplace experiences is institutionally limited, the proactive search for individually applicable synergies between specialization and versatility can be seriously hampered.

In response, one might argue that in a monopolistically rigidified market, it is pointless to pursue a protean career anyway, as working for one of the politically well-entrenched businesses is a surefire recipe for occupational stability and security. However, one should bear in mind that while the businesses in question do enjoy special political protection, the same cannot be said for their individual employees. Thus, as soon as they are dismissed from their occupationally privileged positions, their professional situation may deteriorate particularly rapidly if they inhabit what, barring insulated pockets of monopolistic ossification, is at least a semi-proactive society. More specifically, under such circumstances, they might find it extra difficult to establish several distinct and mutually reinforcing streams of personal productivity characteristic of proactive job seekers, which further compounds the problem of wages potentially being artificially bid below their marginal productivity in a politically fossilized business environment (Méra, 2010).

That being said, it might well be the case that a society that enters at least the initial stage of the transition between the managerial and the proactive form may generate a momentum of ideological changes sufficient to prevent the monopolistic ossification of the economy from taking place. As mentioned in Chapter 1, Section 1.4, several pertinent developments may contribute to this result, including greater political awareness associated with the shift toward non-automatable, human-centered jobs and competences; greater use of the voice option associated with the proliferation of proxy-entrepreneurship; and greater use of the exit option associated with the ascendancy of the protean career model. Taken together, all these phenomena stand a serious chance of diminishing the influence of rent-seeking, including the kind focused on the procurement of government-sponsored monopoly privileges. In other words, the same processes that initially necessitate the emergence of a proactive society may turn out to be an exceptionally effective safeguard against its slide into clientelist politicization.

Finally, it bears mentioning that, especially in view of the preceding remarks concerning the strict relationship between value subjectivity and the nature of entrepreneurial profit, reflecting on the broader consequences of social proactivity can enrich one's understanding of the character of market competition. More specifically, instead of regarding competition as necessarily contributive to the dynamism, innovativeness, and restlessness of the surrounding social milieu, one might just as well see it as a force capable of creating pockets of peace, calm, and predictability for those willing to opt out of what they deem a rat race. The bottom line here is that the latter proposition is by no means anticompetitive. On the contrary, by expanding the range of available sociocultural environments – for instance, in the form of appropriately restrictive covenant communities – it falls squarely into the domain of productive institutional entrepreneurship (Henrekson and Sanandaji, 2011).

That being said, as the above observation puts us in close contact with the subject of welfare and distribution, let us postpone its further exposition until the next section, whose main focus will be precisely this field.

2.4 Welfare and distribution in the proactive society

It might be argued that distribution theory in its earliest formulations, epitomized by Ricardianism, had a distinctly deterministic flavor: it aimed not only at the establishment of the conceptual definitions of various groups of income earners but also at the discovery of the inexorable laws that dictate the respective shares of wealth enjoyed by these groups.

This way of approaching the issue was broadly rejected as a result of advances such as the marginalist theory of value, the time preference theory of interest, and the entrepreneurial market process theory (Rothbard, 1995b: chs. 3–4). Subsequently, the search for deterministic laws of distribution was largely replaced by the inquiry into the logical essence of various kinds of income, treated not so much as empirically precise market phenomena, but as analytically cogent "non-precisive" abstractions (Long, 2006).

More explicitly realistic analyses of this kind, however, emphasize the fact that in the operation of actually existing economies, various categories of income earners are frequently combined or even inextricably intertwined. For instance, in a noninflationary environment characterized by steady capital accumulation and mature financial markets, wage-earning workers can consistently increase their savings rates and easily channel their monetary assets into interest-bearing instruments, thereby becoming capitalists in the proper sense of the term. Likewise, real-world markets do not admit of any strict distinction between capitalists and entrepreneurs, as the former, in committing their resources to investment purposes, have to exhibit the entrepreneurial ability of penetrating the veil of uncertainty, while the latter, in virtue of launching business ventures, have to display the capitalist trait of delaying immediate gratification (Salerno, 2008).

In view of the observations made in the preceding sections of the present chapter, in the proactive society, such categorial crossovers are likely to be significantly more frequent and multifaceted than those existing in its caste-based or managerially driven predecessors. For example, a hired employee who advances to the role of proxy-entrepreneur can collect income that combines regular wages associated with fulfilling routine tasks and quasi-profits associated with instances of self-starting problem identification, intrapreneurial initiative, and other forms of semi-independent value creation for the company. Similarly, a regular worker who is also an individual shareholder of the firm he works for can collect income that combines normal wages with capital gains earned through positively impacting the value of the said firm's products as an activist consumer or a prosumer-innovator. Finally, a seasoned pursuer of a protean career can expect his income to consist not just of standard wages but also of quasi-rents stemming from his possession of unique human and social capital.

In sum, contemplating the character of the proactive society does not necessitate any fundamental rethinking of the classical marginalist-subjectivist theory of distribution, but it allows for its analytical elaboration and more nuanced application. In other words, it does not call for any reconsideration of the logical essence of particular categories of income, but it casts a more penetrating light on their complex interrelations that emerge under specific institutional conditions (Hodgson, 2019).

Furthermore, the "interstitial" nature of the distribution of income in the proactive society provides a telling illustration of the marginal theory of factor pricing by pointing out that exhibiting various forms of proactivity can boost one's income insofar as it involves offering multiple kinds of factor services. This, in turn, furnishes a striking demonstration of the contention that in a catallactic order, production and distribution are two sides of the same coin, both being determined by sovereign consumer wants and the abilities of productive factor owners to satisfy them. Thus, patterns of mutually beneficial catallactic cooperation turn out to be the obverse of patterns of valuable resource allocation (Buchanan, 1982).

Now, the next crucial question to ask is the following one: if, on the one hand, we are to agree that a consistent application of the subjectivist theory of value implies the impossibility of making interpersonal comparisons of utility, and, on the other hand, we wish to remain within the confines of value-free economics, what conclusions should we draw from the above theory of distribution with regard to the theory of welfare?

One noteworthy answer to this question, which unambiguously subscribes to the above two stipulations, suggests that the only states of affairs that can be reliably classified as Pareto-superior are those that stem from voluntarily demonstrated preferences of transactional participants (Rothbard, 1956; Herbener, 1997). Now, on the one hand, this is a very modest analytical proposition, which says nothing more than that every uncoerced transaction constitutes a "plain state of rest", whereby all mutual gains from trade are temporarily exhausted (Klein, 2008: 172). On the other hand, however, as soon as we combine this proposition with the "proactive" theory of distribution sketched in the preceding paragraphs, we may conclude that from the transactional point of view, welfare gains are proportional to the number of distinct functional roles performed by the exchanging parties.

This, of course, raises the immediate problem of how such disparate roles are to be ranked in terms of their welfare-enhancing ability, but one obvious way to dispose of this difficulty is simply to suggest that the greater the number of such roles that are successfully exhibited in a given act, the greater its potential for consumer satisfaction. That is to say, an individual who engages in value creation both as a regular employee and as a proxy-entrepreneur or a prosumer-innovator can be said to create value in more areas than an individual who carries out exclusively standard workplace routines.

The above point can be further amplified when combined with the proactively oriented value theory discussed in one of the previous sections of the present chapter. According to the theory in question, it is not the degree of closeness to the never-never world of final equilibrium that should be regarded as the proper criterion of economic welfare, but rather the degree to which a given act enlarges the scale and scope of viable social cooperation. In this connection, it appears an uncontroversial conclusion that the number of distinct functional roles performed by a given agent is directly correlated with his ability to make such cooperation more broad and qualitatively multifaceted. To illustrate this claim with a simple example grounded in the well-known Smithian dictum that the division of labor is limited by the extent of the market, it seems clear that employees who confront novel business contingencies as proxy-entrepreneurs or offer constructive business feedback as prosumer-innovators make the market more extensive, responsive, and fine-grained than their passively reactive and managerially restricted counterparts.

A similar contention can also be reinforced by combining the presently discussed welfare criterion with the proactively oriented capital theory elaborated earlier. Among other things, this theory allows one to appreciate the fact that proactivity can operate on various levels of the economy-wide capital structure of production, including not only that of "playing the game" but also that of setting the "rules of the game". In other words, proactive behavior can involve not only creating unique configurations of capital assets in the face of singular sets of circumstances but also establishing institutional environments in which such resource-based creativity becomes particularly feasible or even possible at all (Leeson and Boettke, 2009; Boettke, 2014). Thus, an agent, who collects special ownership rents on account of being a skillful owner-manager, earns entrepreneurial profits on account of being a successful uncertainty bearer, and pockets an additional institutional premium on account of creating a favorable milieu for new forms of socioeconomic collaboration, can be said to engage in three distinct, mutually reinforcing forms of welfare improvement in virtue of operating on three distinct but interrelated institutional levels.

In sum, so far, I have tried to argue that a proactively aligned understanding of Pareto-superiority allows for a rough gradation of transactional efficiency gains based on the number of simultaneous collaborative functions carried out by a given actor. At this point, however, one might suggest that no analytical enrichment of welfare theory inspired by the advent of the proactive society can be justifiably regarded as logically complete unless one takes into consideration the fate of those who are not proactive and find it insurmountably challenging to change in this respect. In other words, one might argue that all of the welfare gains associated with the widespread emergence of employee self-directedness, proxy-entrepreneurship, prosumer innovativeness, protean career-building, and similar phenomena may be more than offset by the corresponding welfare losses accruing to those who are chronically incapable of acquiring the proactive skillset. If utility is to be treated as interpersonally incomparable, then, one might add, the disutility accruing to the non-proactive part of society leaves the issue of net welfare gains in this context indeterminate at best.

In response, one might appeal to what has been said in the preceding sections about the nature of value and capital, as seen through the lenses of the proactive framework. First, as a consistently subjectivist approach to the process of valuation does not put any constraints on the set of desirable goods and services, economic growth and development need not necessarily be identified with technological progress, business dynamism, career mobility, and other standard indicators of economic vitality. Instead, they might just as well be identified with the increasing ability of individuals to self-select into independent communities governed in accordance with specific sets of fixed traditions and codes of conduct. That is to say, an important element of social and economic proactivity might consist in the efforts of institutional entrepreneurs aimed at establishing ever more qualitatively diverse and custom-tailored "social spaces" (Storr, 2008).

Second, in view of what has been said earlier regarding the nature of higher-order proactivity geared toward the creation of institutional arrangements capable of enlivening "dead human capital", it might be argued that even traditionally oriented people who find themselves in a self-governing environment of like-minded individuals can become genuinely proactive in their own right. More specifically, they can display great personal initiative in making a dormant tradition flourish or adapting what purports to be a timeless code of conduct to a unique set of local circumstances. Thus, they can tellingly demonstrate that cultivating long-established cultural norms need not be necessarily opposed to organizational ingenuity and social dynamism. On the contrary, such phenomena may indicate that the adherents of a given tradition have skin in the game when it comes to its active maintenance instead of remaining on the level of empty verbal commitments (Taleb, 2018).

Finally, the foregoing considerations allow for formulating an additional argument against the claim that the welfare theory grounded in the criterion of voluntarily demonstrated preferences is fatally vitiated by the existence of unobservable psychological externalities such as envy. What might be called the standard answer to this objection is that such externalities can be alleged to accompany every conceivable transaction, but such contentions have no bearing on the propositions of scientific economics, which focuses on actual results of human action divorced from speculative psychologizing on the underlying motives and concomitant feelings (Herbener, 2008: 66–67). However, an alternative reply, which might be seen as an attempt to accommodate the influence of such intangible external effects, might suggest that institutionally creative proactivity increases social welfare, among other reasons, precisely because it defuses envy on account of allowing for the emergence of multiple simultaneous and incommensurable standards of social success.

In other words, insofar as individuals can self-select into communities whose criteria of merit are consistent with the formers' specific skillsets and the corresponding cultural preferences, they are unlikely to exhibit envy understood as the feeling that others are undeserving of their superior material or social standing. By the same token, they are unlikely to believe that they are entitled to appropriate someone else's belongings or position, which could otherwise prompt them to support purely redistributive, zero-sum policies (Schoeck, 1987).

The above observation highlights some unobvious, but important connections between welfare theory and the theory of competition. More specifically, it emphasizes the fact that what might be called higher-order competition – that is, that between institutional settings rather than between business entities – can lead to welfare increases in virtue of accommodating the preferences of individuals eager to live in what would be traditionally understood as non-competitive cultural environments. That is to say, the contention that competition is a discovery procedure (Hayek, 2002) can be meaningfully applied not only to "playing the social game" but to determining its rules as well, with the latter implying that there is no single way in which the "game" in question has to be played. By the same token, demonstrating a preference for living in a specific institutional and cultural milieu can be as much of a Pareto-superior outcome as demonstrating a preference for a specific good or service offered within that milieu.

In concluding the present section, it bears mentioning that the potential for welfare increases associated with the advent of the proactive society can be effectively tapped into in view of the latter's organizational, political, ethical, and cognitive characteristics described in the previous chapter.

First, as pointed out in Section 1.3, as the proactive society is likely to consist of a large number of relatively small firms, and as firms can be justifiably regarded as constitutional orders in their own right, demonstrating preferences for living and working under particular forms of genuinely contractual governance is bound to become exceptionally effortless under such structural arrangements. This is especially so, given the fact that businesses willing to become lastingly attractive to proactive employees need to be able to establish culturally intimate environments that allow for expressing strong value commitments, which requires being adept not just at narrowly defined market entrepreneurship but at institutional entrepreneurship as well (Abrutyn and Van Ness, 2015).

Second, as noted in Section 1.4, widespread proactive orientation is likely to aid the effective use of voice and exit options; reduce the impact of rational ignorance and rational irrationality; help solve collective action problems in the face of the entrenched influence of special interest groups; and promote other activities conducive to political decentralization, direct self-governance, and related forms of institutional self-selection and organizational unanimity. This, in turn, promises to result in welfare gains generated by means of purely voluntary (and thus clearly mutually beneficial) transactions conducted not only on, to borrow a central distinction from public choice theory, the "post-constitutional level" but on the "constitutional level" as well. That is to say, proactively driven political fragmentation into independent communities of constitutionally like-minded individuals can bring about, to use another vital public choice distinction, actual as opposed to merely "conceptual" unanimity regarding the acceptance of the binding "rules of the game" (Wiśniewski, 2017).

Third, as indicated in Section 1.5, insofar as the proactive society can be expected to enjoy a higher level of productivity and wealth than its more managerially oriented predecessors, its members, overly satiated with purely material and entertainment-based amenities, may increasingly demand more ethically and culturally tinged goods, including those capable of serving as catalysts of robust bonding capital. This, in turn, may create ample opportunities for multilevel entrepreneurs skilled not only at producing highbrow, "socially conscious", or culturally embedded goods but also at building or reinforcing institutional frameworks within which the production of such goods can flourish, especially inasmuch as community development through equity distribution is involved (Kotha and George, 2012).

In addition, ethical fastidiousness coupled with financial abundance may cause an increasing number of ordinary employees operating in the proactive society to assume the role of activist consumer-investors willing to co-create the social and normative strategies of the companies they work for. As under such circumstances, making the strategies in question strictly attuned to the moral demands of customers may serve as one of the chief sources of lasting competitive advantage, becoming an activist consumer-investor of the kind discussed here, far from generating mere moralistic nuisance, can genuinely boost a company's profitability in virtue of broadening its vision of value creation and enhancing its capacity for consumer empowerment (Hirsto, 2011).

Finally, as suggested in Section 1.6, one of the primary challenges of harnessing the cognitive potential of the proactive society is to deal successfully with the disorienting influence of information overload. In order to do so, entrepreneurs may need to establish structures of corporate governance within which mandatory procedures are relatively few in number and maximally transparent, while the degree of employee discretion is substantial, thus combining informational authority and informational self-management in optimal proportions. This, in turn, implies that multilevel entrepreneurs, who engage in value creation on several institutional levels, may be particularly capable of bringing about welfare increases in virtue of building not only well-functioning corporate environments but also autonomous sociocultural communities whose small size and intimate atmosphere allow for prudent, self-directed filtering of information flows (Jones, Ravid, and Rafaeli, 2004).

Furthermore, one especially fruitful strategy of avoiding consumer information overload may consist in focusing one's attention primarily on those goods and services whose productive attributes can be feasibly influenced by prosumer-style innovative tinkering. Such tinkering, when coupled with detailed and compelling consumer feedback, might eventually be incorporated by appropriately responsive entrepreneurs into their original offerings, thereby turning prosumer-innovators who hold shares in the relevant companies into successful retail activist investors. In other words, insofar as the proactive society encourages the expansion of creative prosumerism, it allows satisfied clients living in it to enjoy dual welfare gains: those grounded in the use value of purchased items as well as those associated with the growing capital value of the firms that produce them (Lombardo and Cabiddu, 2017).

To conclude, the acquisition of insights into the nature of the distribution of income offered by the advent of the proactive society goes hand in hand with the unleashing of the potential for welfare increases that is unique to the socioeconomic system in question. It goes without saying, however, that putting those insights into practice and tapping into this potential successfully may require novel reflection on the desired professional competences of truly productive individuals, thus possibly necessitating a reconsideration of the definition of labor, the composition of the labor force, and the meaning of unemployment. It is to these issues that I intend to turn in the next section.

2.5 Employment and labor in the proactive society

In view of what has been said in the foregoing paragraphs about the defining characteristics of the proactive society, it can be concluded that the employment relation in such a socioeconomic environment is bound to be much less strictly defined, far more open-ended, and vastly more changeable over time than it is likely to be under managerial, feudal, despotic or even early capitalist conditions.

Several pertinent factors bear mentioning in this connection. First, the ascendancy of widespread automation inexorably pushes human beings in the direction of tasks whose successful completion requires specifically interpersonal competences. This, in turn, makes job descriptions less technically determinate, as they increasingly involve dealing with at least some exposure to Knightian uncertainty, black swan-type events, and other phenomena associated with the presence of unique scenarios. Second, the growing importance of proxy-entrepreneurship necessitates that even rank and file employees become capable of displaying Schumpeterian innovativeness, Kirznerian alertness, and other characteristically entrepreneurial traits as part of their workplace routines. Finally, the pursuit of protean careers necessarily results in the occupational histories of the majority of workers becoming progressively variegated and multidisciplinary.

The above observations allow for formulating novel insights into the nature of various traditionally defined categories of unemployment. For instance, it appears likely that in the proactive society, frictionally unemployed individuals would be eager to adopt a significantly more dynamic approach to occupational change than they do today, especially in connection with making the leap from proxy-entrepreneurship to full-blooded firm ownership. More specifically, instead of simply taking time to survey the existing professional landscape, such individuals might seek out opportunities to gain inside knowledge about the operation of successful companies in various industries. In doing so, they might, for example, take personalized quasi-internships based on shadowing high-level executives, attend numerous shareholder meetings, converse with managerial and technical specialists in their occupational habitats, etc.

Needless to say, as such "experiential internships" (Varghese et al., 2012) require devoting substantial attention to the "trainees" and allowing them to gain an intimate understanding of specialized business environments, one can expect them to be paid rather than free. This may suggest that their beneficiaries should, for all practical purposes, be treated as students and thus as individuals who are outside of the labor force rather than unemployed. However, given the decidedly commercial nature of such seemingly educational undertakings and their strict entrepreneurial orientation, such a classification of their pursuers might be regarded as problematic. This is why it might be more advisable to designate them as "frictionally unemployed students" or "temporarily unemployed continuous learners", thereby emphasizing the increasingly intertwined nature of continuous education and professional advancement in the proactive society.

The foregoing remarks also allow for the realization that interventionism aimed at stimulating or rigidifying the labor market is bound to turn the abovementioned educational variety of frictional unemployment into its particularly harmful structural counterpart. This is due to the fact that the survival of the proactive society requires the market-wide structure of human capital to be exceptionally well-integrated and internally consistent so as to satisfy the variegated wants of fastidious customers. This, in turn, implies that labor market interventions – for instance, in the form of artificial credit expansion or minimum wage legislation – distort this structure by divorcing it from freely demonstrated preferences of sovereign consumers and voluntary savers, thereby generating persistent skill mismatches and boom-bust cycles followed by periods of jobless recovery (Burns, 2018).

Such distortions can be expected to be especially damaging to the pursuers of protean careers, including those who aim at transitioning from being hired employees to full-scale entrepreneurs, as they not only impede the process of gathering appropriately multifaceted and complementary professional experiences but also encourage gathering experiences which, while seemingly profitable at first glance, ultimately turn out to have been undertaken on the basis of misleading price signals, thus resulting in deep structural maladjustments in the labor force. Even more strikingly, reflecting on the nature of structural unemployment in the proactive society drives home the point that, judged from the perspective of building the long-term value of one's personal human capital, being frictionally or even cyclically unemployed is preferable to being protractedly malemployed during an artificial boom, particularly one that is repeatedly reinflated. This realization also tellingly illustrates the more general point that the purpose of a well-functioning economy is not to achieve the unfeasible goal of "full employment" but to facilitate the maximum level of actually productive employment, which may well coincide with regular periods of speculative and educational joblessness on the part of many of the most ambitious members of the labor force.

The above considerations provide additional arguments for the fairly uncontroversial contention that being in the state of temporary professional idleness need not imply being economically unproductive and unconcerned with one's future earnings prospects. However, envisioning the workings of the proactive society also allows for substantiating a somewhat more unusual conclusion – namely, the view that exhibiting exclusively "passive" productivity should not place one outside of the conventionally defined labor force. So-called rentiers are typically excluded from it because their income is said to be derived entirely from the occupational activities of others – that is, those tasked with enhancing the value of the capital entrusted to them. And yet, one might argue that in an economic environment that places a particular premium on proactivity, the amount of intellectual labor that needs to be done if one is to become a successful rentier is quite substantial.

More specifically, as indicated in the section on capital theory, insofar as the emergence of the proactive society goes hand in hand with the intensification of wealth-enhancing phenomena such as worker empowerment, prosumer innovativeness, and entrepreneurial emancipation, the loan markets existing in it are likely to be awash with private savings. Consequently, in such a milieu, the return on low-risk investment vehicles, including bank deposits and savings accounts, can be expected to be increasingly inconsequential. Furthermore, passive index investing treated as the default option for risk-averse retail investors can plausibly lead to the emergence of asset bubbles whereby ever more individuals pile growing amounts of money into a strictly limited set of high-capitalization stocks (Laborda, Laborda, and de la Cruz, 2024). In other words, if a mass scramble for a finite number of property titles is generally regarded as a safe method of benefiting from the steady development of the economy, the resulting financial activities are bound to generate a self-defeating prophecy in which everyone's attempt to capitalize on a desirable attribute of a given asset brings about its destruction.

Thus, the kind of proactivity that enlarges the pool of savings available to retail investors necessitates the emergence of another kind of proactivity: that associated with the ability to spot situations in which a recklessly passive approach to certain financial instruments divorces them from the underlying fundamentals, consequently calling for corrective interventions by active speculators. That is to say, the pursuit of capital gains in the proactive society brings a particular clarity to the realization that passive investing is not necessarily less risky and easier to diversify than its active counterpart and may actually be less promising on both of these fronts when the companies that comprise the main stock market indices become oversaturated liquidity sponges. As one can readily surmise, this realization derives from the fact that, at the end of the day, identifying a genuinely low-risk and well-diversified set of financial assets has to be a result of personal initiative and individual insight (De Jong and Rhee, 2008). Following the crowd into the "default option", on the other hand, no matter how appealing it may look like, always runs the major risk of being self-defeating in virtue of diluting the competitive edge of the proposition under consideration. By the same token, it is a paradigmatic example of non-proactive behavior in the realm of personal finance.

Another group typically excluded from the labor force that deserves being commented on in connection with the advent of widespread proactivity are the retirees. The strongest thesis that one can formulate here is that in the proactive society, the concept of retirement should be retired altogether (Dychtwald, Erickson, and Morison, 2004), as self-starting and initiative-driven individuals abhor the prospect of becoming permanently unproductive in the latter stage of their lives.

This abhorrence can be theorized to be particularly amplified by three main factors. First, the same technological advancement that leads to the automation of the majority of routine tasks, thereby pushing employees in the direction of specifically human-related activities, can be plausibly regarded as prolonging their period of good health on account of offering them increasingly invigorating nutritional, medicinal, and therapeutic solutions. Second, the growing role of proxy-entrepreneurship, which is by definition detached from the repetitive grind of exhausting physical toil, allows even rank and file workers to focus primarily on mentally rather than bodily demanding goals, thus enabling them to preserve their good health and their professional energy for much longer than used to be the case. And third, getting used to the pursuit of protean careers, which requires the ability to stay alert to the most promising job opportunities on offer at any given time, maximizes the chances of sticking to the kinds of occupations that one finds not just financially rewarding but also all-around satisfying and hence unlikely to deplete one's productive potential.

In sum, a number of coinciding factors associated with the environment of pervasive proactivity may result in the majority of people staying economically productive for the entirety of their post-education lives. Even those, however, who decide to leave full-time employment upon reaching sufficiently advanced age may remain fruitful members of the proactive society in virtue of working part-time jobs, undertaking short-term contracts, and engaging in other forms of "bridge employment" (Zhan and Wang, 2014). And as the gold standard of productivity in the proactive society is not procedural knowledge or narrow technical expertise but personal initiative, creative adaptability, entrepreneurial acumen, and other such strictly experience-based skills and capabilities, the continued (even if partial) presence of seasoned employees in the workforce may be particularly conducive to the intergenerational transfer of this crucial know-how.

Thus, in a milieu of widespread proactivity, it becomes at least a dubious proposition to automatically downgrade the projected productivity of the economy in response to an increase in the number and proportion of retirees who inhabit it. As stated above, this is due to the fact that in such a setting, it might be uniquely easy to coax professionally accomplished individuals out of retirement, keep them occupationally busy on a part-time basis, and derive exceptional benefits from the advice and insight of even those among them who decide to remain permanently out of the workforce.

Finally, the foregoing considerations can be said to shed new light on the very definition of labor and especially on the claim that labor necessarily implies some form of disutility. Thus, for instance, it is often proposed that labor is inherently unpleasant on the physical or psychological level, which discourages employees from expending their full productive capacity during any given work period. While admittedly this may be the case with the majority of currently existing occupations, especially those of a highly mechanical and repetitive character, the same conclusion need not apply to the professional landscape of the proactive society, where a special premium is placed on human-centric skills that allow for dealing with unique challenges, singular problems, and uncertain contingencies. Under such conditions, where fulfilling one's occupational duties is likely to provide a potentially inexhaustible supply of intellectual gratification and emotional thrill, labor may be more likely than not to offer not just extrinsic benefits in the form of monetary remuneration but also intrinsic benefits in the form of genuine personal development.

An alternative formulation of the reasons for the existence of the disutility of labor suggests that they consist in the fact that leisure is labor's inevitable opportunity cost (Fegley and Israel, 2020). Hence, even in those cases where a given job is associated with intrinsic satisfaction on the part of its performers, its mutual exclusivity with enjoying leisure time is supposed to bring about an ineradicable quantum of disutility.

As plausible as it might seem on the empirical level, this contention appears to miss the mark insofar as it fails to establish a logically necessary truth. After all, one might well imagine, say, an accomplished multitasker who conducts major business dealings while simultaneously relishing the sumptuous atmosphere of industry banquets and other prestigious corporate events (Salerno, 2020). In other words, the person under consideration might well be capable of achieving a seamless intratemporal combination of labor and leisure. This, however, is still congruent with refraining from expending one's full productive capacity, as at some point, the diminishing marginal utility of even the most intrinsically pleasant and leisure-compatible kind of work is bound to be overtaken by the increasing marginal utility of the unconsumed fruits of one's efforts.

Thus, even in an environment of pervasive proactivity, one cannot expect even the most satisfied employees to work up until the moment of complete physical and mental exhaustion. That being said, nonetheless, the preceding remarks emphasize that the way to obtain a workforce-based competitive advantage in the proactive society is to entice prospective jobholders with positions that promise to be intrinsically rewarding and potentially immune to the trade-off between labor and leisure. Such positions, one might argue, are particularly likely to bring out their holders' ability to identify novel problems in advance, engage in proxy-entrepreneurship, multitask creatively and successfully, and exercise other forms of self-starting initiative by means of regularly stimulating flow-like experiences (Csikszentmihalyi and LeFevre, 1989).

This observation provides yet another instance of the general phenomenon discussed throughout the present chapter, whereby in the proactive society, various analytically distinct and conceptually separable economic categories exhibit a tendency toward coexistence and mutual reinforcement. That is to say, just as a satisfied and highly inquisitive consumer can turn into a prosumer-innovator, thereby combining the use value of the consumed good with the potential exchange value of the constructive feedback offered to its producer, and just as an experienced pursuer of a protean career can be regarded as a quasi-entrepreneur insofar as he needs to manage actively his unique set of human capital assets, an employee involved in a task exceptionally suited to his personal interests and ambitions may well consider his occupation as a leisurely endeavor in the proper sense of the term.

Such a conclusion, in turn, suggests that not only labor and productivity but perhaps also the more general concepts of rationality and efficiency can be seen in a broader and brighter light when looked at from the perspective of agents operating in a proactive society. Let us explore this issue in the next and final section of the present chapter.

2.6 Rationality and efficiency in the proactive society

Rationality can be justifiably regarded as one of the most perennially contested concepts in the realm of economic theory. Those methodological traditions that conceive of rationality in the broadest possible terms consider it as identical with purposiveness, that is, the ability to select consciously the goals that promise to bring the agent the greatest amount of utility and the means that the agent deems as maximally conducive to the attainment of those goals (Wiśniewski, 2009). According to this view, calling human action "rational" is pleonastic, as it is necessarily intentional, as opposed to, say, animal and plant behavior. On the other hand, those traditions that subscribe to a more narrow and substantive understanding of rationality – including most notably the neoclassical mainstream – see it as a characteristic of only those actions that are performed by agents endowed with sufficient cognitive resources and skills such as "full information", resistance to behavioral biases, perfect foresight, and the ability to perform numerically precise utility calculations in all conceivable choice situations (Ceolin and Mazzoni, 2024).

Now, while it appears clear that the former conception of rationality is more closely attuned to how real-life human agents pursue their goals in the world of ineradicable scarcity and pervasive uncertainty, its analytical breadth may ultimately be more suited to developing pure economic theory than to analyzing the skillsets that are necessary for thriving under particular socio-economic conditions. In other words, while identifying rationality with purposiveness allows for deriving the law of demand, the law of diminishing marginal utility, and similar fundamental economic principles from sound reflection on the nature of human action, it offers no direct guidance regarding the features of activities whose successful operation is crucial for the maintenance of complex and specialized systems of social cooperation.

As the proactive society is clearly an example of such a system, a cogent description of its workings requires the assumption that a substantial number of its members display at least the kind of rationality that is more than mere intentionality, though it can be far less than the quasi-omniscience and computational mastery stipulated in overly stylized neoclassical models. In fact, proactivity can be defined as precisely the middle ground form of rationality that is neither a necessary characteristic of all action nor a characteristic of actions performed exclusively by neoclassical utility maximizers, but rather the essential feature of individuals capable of exercising various facets of the entrepreneurial mindset, even without being entrepreneurs in the full sense of the term.

In keeping with its designation as a middle ground concept, rationality-as-proactivity should be thought of neither as an inherent attribute of all human beings (in contrast to purposiveness) nor as the sole hallmark of robotically calculative decision-makers (in contrast to the ability to engage in neoclassical-style optimization), but as a generally achievable characteristic that can be developed and honed on the basis of training, experience, and dedication. That is to say, while it would be unreasonable to expect the majority of the members of any given society to ascend to the position of full-fledged entrepreneurs (if only for the reason of the necessarily complementary roles of employers and employees), it appears eminently plausible to envision a community whose every member is at least rudimentarily capable of advance problem identification, self-starting exploration of possible solutions to novel challenges, and other operations typical of broadly conceived "men of action" (D'Andrea, 2024).

The crucial point to be noted here is that the various conceptions of rationality mentioned above are analytically complementary rather than mutually exclusive. The most extensive of them – purposiveness – allows for identifying exceptionless causal connections between various elements of the structure of human action, the narrowest of them – optimization – enables to single out cognitive biases that prevent specific instances of human action from reaching their intended goals, while the intermediate one – proactivity – enumerates skills and competences whose widespread presence is indispensable in environments where social cooperation progresses successfully beyond a critical threshold of technological complexity, organizational specialization, and professional dynamism.

In other words, the concept of rationality-as-proactivity appears particularly useful in the context of analyzing the unfolding of the cooperative potential of human action in increasingly advanced and demanding socioeconomic frameworks. As such, it seems exceptionally capable of establishing a bridge between the development of pure economic theory and its application to the real-world market process and its broader social ramifications.

This, in turn, implies that the concept in question is likely to be especially useful in advancing economics as seen through the lens of the "exchange paradigm" rather than that of the "allocation paradigm" (Buchanan, 1964) – that is, in advancing economics understood as the science of social collaboration, not as the science of individual choice. This conclusion appears only natural as soon as we realize that rationality-as-purposiveness can be exhibited even by Robinson Crusoe choosing between different methods of obtaining food on his desert island, while rationality-as-optimization can be exhibited by his computationally brilliant and perfectly informed, but equally isolated counterpart. Rationality-as-proactivity, on the other hand, can be successfully deployed only in multi-agent environments, which, as such, are necessarily characterized by the presence of uncertainty, behavioral novelty, transaction costs, and other specifically social phenomena. In other words, proactivity turns out to be an important type of "ecological rationality" (Smith, 2003), that is, the crucial feature that allows individuals to pursue their goals ever more effectively in virtue of integrating themselves in an increasingly productive manner into specific ecosystems of social relations and institutions.

One should notice in this connection that some such ecosystems promote the acquisition of the cognitive skills characteristic of those who are commonly referred to as "rational agents", while others discourage their development or even attract those who conspicuously lack them. For instance, it has been noted that monetary systems that make generous use of artificial credit expansion induce relatively imprudent entrepreneurs to engage in capital-intensive business projects while causing their more prudent counterparts to remain on the sidelines or even liquidate their current investments (Engelhardt, 2012). Thus, in such environments, assets are routinely reallocated from rational to irrational enterprises, with predictably ruinous results. On the other hand, monetary systems reliant on traditional commodity standards and full reserve banks, where the amount of available credit is strictly determined by the social savings rate, impose stringent limits on who can become a beneficiary of a business loan, thereby ensuring that scarce financial resources remain in the hands of comparatively proficient businesspeople.

Likewise, socioeconomic milieus that beguile their prospective inhabitants with promises of guaranteed welfare provisions attract individuals who are particularly prone to learned helplessness and other behavioral habits that constitute the opposite of mature self-reliance and responsible public-mindedness (Murray, 1994). On the other hand, institutional frameworks in which professional, communal, and personal advancement requires displaying various forms of proactivity are likely to attract individuals who are especially capable of and eager to develop and make use of these very characteristics. This, however, need not imply that such frameworks are bound to exclude persons who are not inherently proactive, let alone that they should be regarded as "dog-eat-dog" environments bereft of any concern for the welfare of the needy, as, as indicated in Section 2.4, a significant part of institutional entrepreneurship may consist precisely in the gratuitous provision of professional training and behavioral know-how aimed at unleashing the proactive potential of dispositionally reactive individuals.

In sum, rationality-as-proactivity is a phenomenon that fits naturally the understanding of the market process as the bedrock of "dynamic efficiency" (Huerta de Soto, 2008), that is, the feature whereby the beneficiaries of large-scale social cooperation tend to become increasingly adept at satisfying the needs of their fellow human beings, or else they are progressively deprived of its fruits. In other words, rationality conceived in this sense is neither an automatic virtue possessed by every purposive agent nor an exclusive privilege of the narrow "cognitive elite", but a trait whose determined pursuit is catalyzed by the market and whose persistent neglect is penalized by the market (List and Millimet, 2008). Thus, the proactive concept of rationality appears uniquely fruitful in illuminating not the content of general economic laws or the prerequisites of solutions to specific economic problems, but the entrepreneurial, processual dynamism characteristic of sustained economic growth and development.

As in the previous paragraph I referred to the notion of efficiency, which is oftentimes closely connected to the notion of rationality in the context of methodological considerations, let me now comment somewhat more extensively on the former and on the ways in which it can be productively expanded when looked at through the lens of the proactive society.

One distinction that might be particularly useful here is that between technical and economic efficiency. Technical efficiency can be defined as the ability of a given agent to accomplish a given goal successfully along as many objectively ascertainable dimensions as possible, including quickness, comprehensiveness, reliability, and professional quality. Economic efficiency, on the other hand, can be defined as the ability of a given agent to contribute to consumer satisfaction, meaning the capacity to increase the number of available scarce goods and earn the corresponding profit.

The crucial observation to be made here is that these two kinds of efficiency can diverge quite dramatically. To take what is perhaps the most salient example in this connection, communist dictatorships are clearly able to marshal enormous resources to accomplish great feats of political propaganda, such as exceptionally lavish parades and imposingly monumental politburo buildings, but they are nonetheless incapable of engaging in rational economic calculation, as they cannot rely on meaningful price signals generated by private entrepreneurs competing for scarce factors of production (Rothbard, 1991). Likewise, so-called AI algorithms may be proficient at optimizing the use of given data in view of wanting to attain a given end, but they can make no prudent selection among ends geared toward maximum consumer satisfaction, as they possess no theory of mind, thus being unable to exercise authentic entrepreneurial judgment (Phelan, 2020).

In other words, while it seems impossible to be economically efficient without being technically efficient in a specific field, the reverse is certainly conceivable. Hence, the next natural question that arises here is the following one: what institutional, organizational, social, and cultural preconditions need to be present if a solid bridge is to be built between technical and economic efficiency, ensuring that the objective productivity associated with the former is to be subordinated to the subjective value creation associated with the latter?

On a broad level, the answer to this question is already well established – after all, it is a rather uncontroversial contention that no amount of resources, manpower, and know-how can be successfully converted into consumer satisfaction and economic vibrancy in the absence of secure property rights (O'Driscoll and Hoskins, 2003), monetary predictability (Buchanan, 1962), legal certainty (Higgs, 1997), unhampered cost accounting (Mises, 2008), and widespread respect for entrepreneurial activities (McCloskey, 2016). It is less clear, however, how the same conversion can be enacted on the level of the individual and his professional environment, which is typically that of the firm.

Addressing this issue in a satisfactory manner may require invoking the notion of proactivity, treated as the connecting middle ground between routine-based technical competence and full-blooded entrepreneurial acumen. More specifically, while even a highly proactive employee is not ultimately responsible for his firm's profitability or lack thereof – as that depends on the owner-entrepreneur, who strives to make the most value-creative use of the resources at his disposal, including the proactivity of his subordinates – he can nonetheless make a unique direct contribution to its productivity. That is to say, while his technical capacity is defined and circumscribed by the particular role assigned to him as part of the overarching strategy adopted by the owner-entrepreneur, within that role, he can come up with novel ways of improving the company's bottom line by means of formulating self-starting responses to singular occurrences.

In other words, he can, to paraphrase a canonical Smithian phrase, increase the division of labor not so much by extending the market outwardly, but by expanding it inwardly, tapping into his unique personal resources and using them as part of an open-ended and flexible occupational routine. Furthermore, in virtue of combining such routines with those of one's fellow employees endowed with similar discretionary decision-making powers, a proactive agent can demonstrate economic efficiency by unleashing the synergistic potential of "co-intrapreneurship" (Wunderer, 2001), a phenomenon whereby individual workers synthesize their problem-solving initiatives, thus acting like strategic business partners rather than like tightly controlled team members.

In sum, proactively oriented employees can be expected to experiment with the degree to which their technically defined roles allow for proxy-entrepreneurial value creation through confrontation with singular situations and the assembly of unrepeatable combinations of the resources at hand, with the crucial caveat being that their experiments are ultimately subject to economic calculation conducted by owner-entrepreneurs or by the top-level managers empowered by them for this task. As far as this process is operative, technical efficiency can be said to morph into its economic counterpart, with the latter serving as the paramount benchmark of performance.

On this note, I would like to bring to a close my discussion of the various ways in which the concept of proactivity can illuminate a number of fundamental fields of economic analysis. As the theoretical considerations presented in this chapter can be regarded as being guided by the natural unfolding of the cooperative potential of humankind – in this case, the transcending of the limitations of the managerial society – they can be justifiably seen as capable not only of providing a comprehensive description of the process under consideration but also of speeding it up. As such, they can be rightly thought of as both theoretically enlightening and practically relevant, with these two characteristics influencing each other in a mutually reinforcing manner.

That being said, one should keep in mind that the emergence of the proactive society is by no means a foregone outcome. The advancement of social cooperation is in no way a linear or deterministic process, but rather a journey along a winding road punctuated by periods of sudden acceleration and rapid retrogression. What is of particular importance in this connection is the realization that a successful and sustainable transition to the next stage of this process requires a felicitous confluence of numerous factors belonging to several distinct categories. And even if such factors are all present at a given period of time – as seems to have been the case in recent years – they can be easily undermined to such an extent that the transition in question can quickly grind to a halt or even suffer a reversal.

In the next chapter, I shall attempt to identify the most crippling obstacles to the continuing unfolding of the proactive society, hoping that a fuller comprehension of their inhibitory influence with regard to the cooperative prospects of globalized societies will help neutralize their harmful effects. Let me then proceed to discussing their main categories and indicating various ways in which they contribute to the erosion of the proactive mindset and its defining characteristics.

Bibliography

Abrutyn, S., Van Ness, J., 2015. The role of agency in sociocultural evolution: Institutional entrepreneurship as a force of structural and cultural change. Thesis Eleven 127 (1), 52–77.

Acuto, M., 2013. City leadership in global governance. Global Governance 19 (3), 481–498.

Block, W., 2008. Market monopoly is apodictically impossible. Corporate Ownership and Control 5 (3), 385–389.

Boettke, P. J., 2014. Entrepreneurship, and the entrepreneurial market process: Israel M. Kirzner and the two levels of analysis in spontaneous order studies. Review of Austrian Economics 27 (3), 233–247.

Böhm-Bawerk, E., 1949 [1898]. Karl Marx and the Close of His System. Augustus M. Kelley, New York.

Braun, E., 2017. The theory of capital as a theory of capitalism. Journal of Institutional Economics 13 (2), 305–325.

Braun, E., Howden, D., 2017. The rise and fall of the subsistence fund as a resource constraint in Austrian business cycle theory. Review of Austrian Economics 30 (2), 235–249.

Brenk, S., Lüttgens, D., Diener, K., Piller, F., 2019. Learning from failures in business model innovation: Solving decision-making logic conflicts through intrapreneurial effectuation. Journal of Business Economics 89 (8), 1097–1147.

Brooks, A. C., 2008. Social Entrepreneurship: A Modern Approach to Social Value Creation. Pearson Education, Upper Saddle River, NJ.

Buchanan, J. M., 1962. Predictability: The Criterion for a Monetary Constitution. In: Yeager, L. B. (Ed.), In Search of a Monetary Constitution. Harvard University Press, Cambridge, MA, 155–183.

Buchanan, J. M., 1964. What should economists do? Southern Economic Journal 30 (3), 213–222.

Buchanan, J. M., 1982. Order defined in the process of its emergence. Literature of Liberty 5, 7–58.

Burns, S., 2018. Human capital and its structure. Journal of Private Enterprise 33 (2), 33–51.

Ceolin, A. M., Mazzoni, J. F. R., 2024. Beyond rationality: Exploring neoclassical, behavioral, and Austrian approaches to finance. Quarterly Journal of Austrian Economics 27 (3), 1–21.

Cordato, R., 2013. Welfare Economics and Externalities in an Open Ended Universe: A Modern Austrian Perspective. Springer Science & Business Media, New York.

Coyne, C. J., Boettke, P. J., 2006. The role of the economist in economic development. Quarterly Journal of Austrian Economics 19 (1), 47–68.

Csikszentmihalyi, M., LeFevre, J., 1989. Optimal experience in work and leisure. Journal of Personality and Social Psychology 56 (5), 815–822.

D'Andrea, F. M., 2024. Man of action: Murray N. Rothbard's contributions to the theory of entrepreneurship. Quarterly Journal of Austrian Economics 27 (2), 11–38.

De Jong, J., Rhee, S., 2008. Abnormal returns with momentum/contrarian strategies using exchange-traded funds. Journal of Asset Management 9 (4), 289–299.

Desouza, K. C., Awazu, Y., Jha, S., Dombrowski, C., Papagari, S., Baloh, P., Kim, J. Y., 2008. Customer-driven innovation. Research-Technology Management 51 (3), 35–44.

Dychtwald, K., Erickson, T., Morison, B., 2004. It's time to retire retirement. Public Policy and Aging Report 14 (3), 1–28.

Elert, N., Stenkula, M., 2022. Intrapreneurship: Productive and non-productive. Entrepreneurship Theory and Practice 46 (5), 1423–1439.

Engelhardt, L., 2012. Expansionary monetary policy and decreasing entrepreneurial quality. Quarterly Journal of Austrian Economics 15 (2), 172–194.

Erken, H., Donselaar, P., Thurik, R., 2018. Total factor productivity and the role of entrepreneurship. The Journal of Technology Transfer 43 (6), 1493–1521.

Fegley, T., Israel, K. F., 2020. The disutility of labor. Quarterly Journal of Austrian Economics 23 (2), 171–179.

Foss, N. J., Klein, P. G., 2010. Alertness, action, and the antecedents of entrepreneurship. The Journal of Private Enterprise 25 (2), 145–164.

Foss, N. J., Klein, P. G., 2012. Organizing Entrepreneurial Judgment: A New Approach to the Firm. Cambridge University Press, Cambridge.

Garrison, R., 2001. Time and Money: The Macroeconomics of Capital Structure. Routledge, London and New York.

Glavan, B., Anghel, F., Avrigeanu, A., 2010. Public education, market, and human capital formation. Romanian Economic and Business Review 5, 17–22.

Harper, D. A., Endres, A. M., 2010. Capital as a layer cake: A systems approach to capital and its multi-level structure. Journal of Economic Behavior & Organization 74 (1–2), 30–41.

Hayek, F. A., 1948. The Meaning of Competition. In: Individualism and Economic Order. University of Chicago Press, Chicago, IL.

Hayek, F. A., 2002. Competition as a discovery procedure. Quarterly Journal of Austrian Economics 5 (3), 9–23.
Henrekson, M., Sanandaji, T., 2011. The interaction of entrepreneurship and institutions. Journal of Institutional Economics 7 (1), 47–75.
Herbener, J., 1997. The pareto rule and welfare economics. Review of Austrian Economics 10 (1), 70–106.
Herbener, J., 2008. In defense of Rothbardian welfare economics. New Perspectives on Political Economy 4 (1), 53–78.
Higgs, R., 1997. Regime uncertainty: Why the great depression lasted so long and why prosperity resumed after the war. The Independent Review 1 (4), 561–590.
Hilton, M., 2009. Prosperity for All: Consumer Activism in an Era of Globalization. Cornell University Press, Ithaca and London.
Hirsto, H., 2011. Everyday discourses of stock market investing: Searching for investor power and responsibility. Consumption, Markets and Culture 14 (1), 57–77.
Hodgson, G. M., 2019. Austrian economics is still not institutional enough. Advances in Austrian Economics 24, 101–110.
Holcombe, R. G., 2009. Product differentiation and economic progress. Quarterly Journal of Austrian Economics 12 (1), 17–35.
Hoppe, H.-H., 2009. "The yield from money held" reconsidered. New Perspectives on Political Economy 5 (2), 129–136.
Huerta de Soto, J., 2008. The Theory of Dynamic Efficiency. Routledge, London.
Hülsmann, J. G., 2003. Facts and counterfactuals in economic law. Journal of Libertarian Studies 17 (1), 57–102.
Hülsmann, J. G., 2016. Cultural consequences of monetary interventions. Journal des Economistes et des Etudes Humaines 22 (1), 77–98.
Johnson, C. M., Tariq, A., Baker, T. L., 2018. From Gucci to green bags: Conspicuous consumption as a signal for pro-social behavior. Journal of Marketing Theory and Practice 26 (4), 339–356.
Jones, Q., Ravid, G., Rafaeli, S., 2004. Information overload and the message dynamics of online interaction spaces: A theoretical model and empirical exploration. Information Systems Research 15 (2), 194–210.
Joo, B. K., Lim, T., 2009. The effects of organizational learning culture, perceived job complexity, and proactive personality on organizational commitment and intrinsic motivation. Journal of Leadership & Organizational Studies 16 (1), 48–60.
Klamer, A., 2011. Cultural entrepreneurship. Review of Austrian Economics 24 (2), 141–156.
Klein, P. G., 2008. The mundane economics of the Austrian school. Quarterly Journal of Austrian Economics 11 (3), 165–187.
Klein, P. G., 2010. The Capitalist and the Entrepreneur. Ludwig von Mises Institute, Auburn, AL.
Knight, F. H., 1985 [1921]. Risk, Uncertainty and Profit. University of Chicago Press, Chicago.
Kotha, R., George, G., 2012. Friends, family, or fools: Entrepreneur experience and its implications for equity distribution and resource mobilization. Journal of Business Venturing 27 (5), 525–543.

Laborda, J., Laborda, R., de la Cruz, J., 2024. Can ETFs affect US financial stability? A quantile cointegration analysis. Financial Innovation 10 (1), 64.

Leeson, P. T., Boettke, P. J., 2009. Two-tiered entrepreneurship and economic development. International Review of Law and Economics 29 (3), 252–259.

Leitch, C. M., McMullan, C., Harrison, R. T., 2013. The development of entrepreneurial leadership: The role of human, social and institutional capital. British Journal of Management 24 (3), 347–366.

List, J. A., Millimet, D. L., 2008. The market: Catalyst for rationality and filter of irrationality. The BE Journal of Economic Analysis & Policy 8 (1), 1–55.

Lombardo, S., Cabiddu, F., 2017. What's in it for me? Capital, value and co-creation practices. Industrial Marketing Management 61, 155–169.

Long, R. T., 2006. Realism and abstraction in economics: Aristotle and Mises versus Friedman. Quarterly Journal of Austrian Economics 9 (3), 3–23.

McCloskey, D., 2016. Bourgeois Equality: How Ideas, Not Capital or Institutions, Enriched the World. University of Chicago Press, Chicago, IL.

Méra, X., 2010. Factor prices under monopoly for their products. Quarterly Journal of Austrian Economics 13 (1), 48–70.

Mises, L., 2008 [1951]. Profit and Loss. Ludwig von Mises Institute, Auburn, AL.

Murray, C., 1994. Losing Ground: American Social Policy, 1950–1980. 10th Anniversary Edition. Basic Books, New York.

O'Driscoll, G. P., Hoskins, L., 2003. Property rights: The key to economic development. Cato Institute Policy Analysis 482, 1–17.

Packard, M., 2019. Entrepreneurship: Toward the Nirvana state of rest. MISES: Interdisciplinary Journal of Philosophy, Law and Economics 7 (3), 523–544.

Phelan, S., 2020. Can entrepreneurship be learned by intelligent machines? Revista de Instituciones, Ideas y Mercados 69, 57–86.

Prigent-Simonin, A. H., Hérault-Fournier, C., 2005. The role of trust in the perception of the quality of local food products: With particular reference to direct relationships between producer and consumer. Anthropology of Food (4), 1–19.

Rothbard, M. N., 1956. Toward a Reconstruction of Utility and Welfare Economics. In: Sennholz, M. (Ed.), On Freedom and Free Enterprise: Essays in Honor of Ludwig von Mises. Van Nostrand, Princeton, NJ, 224–262.

Rothbard, M. N., 1991. The end of socialism and the calculation debate revisited. Review of Austrian Economics 5 (2), 51–76.

Rothbard, M. N., 1995a. The present state of Austrian economics. Journal des Economistes et des Etudes Humaines 6 (1), 43–90.

Rothbard, M. N., 1995b. Classical Economics: An Austrian Perspective on the History of Economic Thought. Vol. 2. Edward Elgar, Cheltenham.

Roundy, P. T., 2021. On entrepreneurial stories: Tolkien's theory of fantasy and the bridge between imagination and innovation. Business Perspectives and Research 9 (1), 31–45.

Salerno, J. T., 2006. A simple model of the theory of money prices. Quarterly Journal of Austrian Economics 9 (4), 39–55.

Salerno, J. T., 2008. The entrepreneur: Real and imagined. Quarterly Journal of Austrian Economics 11 (3–4), 188–207.

Salerno, J. T., 2018. Are ownership rent and pure profit separate returns to the entrepreneur? Quarterly Journal of Austrian Economics 21 (3), 193–208.
Salerno, J. T., 2020. The disutility of labor: A comment on Fegley and Israel. Quarterly Journal of Austrian Economics 23 (2), 180–191.
Schoeck, H., 1987 [1966]. Envy: A Theory of Social Behaviour. Liberty Press, Indianapolis.
Smith, V. L., 2003. Constructivist and ecological rationality in economics. American Economic Review 93 (3), 465–508.
Soto, H. de, 2000. The Mystery of Capital: Why Capitalism Triumphs in the West and Fails Everywhere Else. Basic Books, New York.
Sørensen, J. F., 2016. Rural-urban differences in bonding and bridging social capital. Regional Studies 50 (3), 391–410.
Stockman, D., 2013. The Great Deformation: The Corruption of Capitalism in America. Public Affairs Press, New York.
Storr, V. H., 2008. The market as a social space: On the meaningful extraeconomic conversations that can occur in markets. Review of Austrian Economics 21 (2–3), 135–150.
Taleb, N., 2018. Skin in the Game: Hidden Asymmetries in Daily Life. Random House, New York.
Varghese, M. E., Parker, L. C., Adedokun, O., Shively, M., Burgess, W., Childress, A., Bessenbacher, A., 2012. Experiential internships: Understanding the process of student learning in small business internships. Industry and Higher Education 26 (5), 357–367.
Wiśniewski, J. B., 2009. Well-informedness and rationality: A philosophical overview. Quarterly Journal of Austrian Economics 12 (3), 43–56.
Wiśniewski, J. B., 2017. Legal polycentrism and contractarianism. Ekonomia – Wroclaw Economic Review 23 (2), 75–82.
Wiśniewski, J. B., 2020a. On the impossibility of intellectual property. Quarterly Journal of Austrian Economics 23 (1), 33–45.
Wiśniewski, J. B., 2020b. Austrian economics as a paradigm of golden mean thinking. New Perspectives on Political Economy 16 (1–2), 39–51.
Wiśniewski, J. B., 2022. The ethical structure of production. Ekonomia – Wroclaw Economic Review 28 (1), 25–38.
Wunderer, R., 2001. Employees as "co-intrapreneurs": A transformation concept. Leadership & Organization Development Journal 22 (5), 193–211.
Zhan, Y., Wang, M., 2014. Bridge Employment: Conceptualizations and New Directions for Future Research. In: Bal, P. M., Kooij, D. T. A. M., Rousseau, D. M. (Eds.), Aging Workers and the Employee-Employer Relationship. Springer International Publishing, Cham.

3 Challenges to the proactive society

3.1 Economic challenges to the proactive society

By now, it has become a cliché to claim that one of the most distinctive features of today's socioeconomic landscape is its unprecedentedly globalized character. And yet, this cliché is nonetheless true, and its implications for the trajectory of social and economic development (or retrogression) are still not fully spelled out. This is especially so inasmuch as the inhabitants of a "global world" have an exceptional capacity to benefit from displaying proactivity and, correspondingly, have the most to lose from being stuck in the reactive mindset or in an institutional environment that promotes it.

To wit, for instance, international economic integration encourages the transborder flow of knowledge, specialization according to comparative advantage, and technological diffusion (Grossman and Helpman, 2015), all of which, in turn, increase the premium placed on the high-quality human capital essential for translating these developments into tangible consumer value. That is to say, they highlight the indispensability of the human factor in adapting formulaic technical procedures to unique contingencies arising in the realm of human action.

Furthermore, economic globalization goes hand in hand with the emergence of complex organizational systems characterized by a high degree of international interdependence. This interdependence, while generating substantial benefits derived from the worldwide division of labor, can nevertheless also lead to destructive domino effects, whereby a cluster of errors made in one node of a cooperative network propagates throughout the entire globe, causing cascading holdups, bankruptcies, and similar disruptive events, especially in the financial area (Friedman and Kraus, 2011). This is why under such conditions, a crucial supervisory function has to be performed by proxy-entrepreneurs, who, in spite of not being the residual claimants of companies and other influential organizations, are nonetheless empowered with discretionary powers to identify operational mistakes committed by their superiors and correct them as they arise. In this connection, one should note that such behavior need not be seen as presumption on the part of proxy-entrepreneurs,

DOI: 10.4324/9781003764557-4

but rather as the intended exercise of their specific role as proactive agents confronted with particular circumstantial blunders and oversights perpetrated on higher levels.

Finally, economic globalization brings in its wake cultural globalization in its manifold forms such as cultural hybridization and syncretization, the emergence of transnational lifestyles, and so forth (Tuncer, 2023). This may significantly contribute to cultural dynamism and the attendant rapidity at which consumer tastes change and shift around. This, in turn, may be a major driving force behind the advent of protean careers, which consist of regular occupational turnarounds aimed at keeping pace with volatile consumer preferences.

In view of the above, all the processes geared toward inhibiting or otherwise disrupting the spontaneous progression of globalization must be seen as antithetical to the development of the proactive society. Thus, tariffs, embargoes, quotas, and other tools of waging trade wars, which rapidly break down economic and social interdependencies between different jurisdictions, should be regarded as particularly devastating in this context, with only open military conflicts being even more ruinous. Moreover, given the close connection between commercial openness and peaceful international relations (Weede, 2004), the erosion of the former should be seen as a credible harbinger of the destruction of the latter, hence creating a potential cascade of increasingly harmful blows to the prospects for flourishing proactivity.

As the division of labor is limited by the extent of the market, and as trade wars result in the fragmentation of the world market, they also result in a slowdown in innovation (Chen, Zhang, and Miao, 2023), thereby reducing the premium associated with the possession of highly qualified human capital and, other things being equal, pushing the labor market in the direction of repetitive tasks and routine-based occupations. This, needless to say, reduces the demand for employee proactivity to a substantial degree.

In addition, the dissolution of the global trade network decreases the extent to which companies can grow in size, scope, and complexity. This makes it difficult for them to expand beyond the threshold at which they can be micromanaged, which, in turn, decreases the demand for proxy-entrepreneurship and other forms of self-starting initiative on the part of employees. Moreover, economic isolationism leads to cultural isolationism, which hinders the diffusion and cross-fertilization of ideas, thereby limiting the number of situations in which frontline workers can display proactivity in virtue of answering uncommon queries, fulfilling unusual requests, and tackling unexpected complaints.

Lastly, trade wars go hand in hand with reduced human mobility (Khanna et al., 2023). As a result, there are fewer opportunities for acquiring skills, competences, and experiences that can serve as complementary assets in one's distinctive structure of human capital. This hinders the task of establishing interdisciplinary bridges that are crucial in developing occupational flexibility – an essential trait in a world of volatile consumer culture, rapid technological advancement, and swift information flows. One should note here that such phenomena would not immediately disappear if the international institutional framework sustaining them were to disintegrate, which would make the inability to maintain career elasticity all the more deleterious for one's economic and social well-being.

Furthermore, if waging a trade war is to be regarded as an attempt at purging the local market of the presence of externally produced goods and the influence of their creators, its internal counterpart can be expected to take the form of pursuing an "industrial policy", whereby political and politically connected entities pick winners and losers in the economic realm. This, one might argue, compounds even further the aforementioned tendencies detrimental to the flourishing of proactivity.

More specifically, as the implementation of industrial policies consists of allocating capital at preferential rates to politically favored enterprises, it distorts the meritocratic incentive structure characteristic of competitive markets and replaces it with a motivational system conducive to corruption, rent-seeking, and other forms of predatory opportunism (DiLorenzo, 1984). Unsurprisingly, this derails the process of "creative destruction", whereby promising inventions are commercialized into pathbreaking innovations, and increasingly supplants productive entrepreneurship with its "nonproductive" and "destructive" equivalents (Baumol, 1990). Consequently, productivity-enhancing technological progress stalls, which reduces the market value of proactivity embedded in non-automatable skills and human-centric capabilities.

Likewise, as the pursuit of industrial policies bears the hallmarks of economic central planning (even if it only aims at directing the private market instead of eliminating it), it prioritizes hierarchical subordination and top-down coordination over spontaneous problem-solving and bottom-up employee engagement. As a result, worker proactivity is bound either to remain untapped or, in the worst-case scenario, to degenerate into perverse forms of intrapreneurship geared toward the discovery and exploitation of novel rent-seeking methods (Elert and Stenkula, 2022).

Next, it should be noticed that the execution of industrial policies necessarily brings in its wake the emergence of classically defined monopolies and oligopolies, that is, business entities or their coalitions that owe their dominant position to the enjoyment of political grants of exclusive privilege (Holcombe, 2013). This, in turn, ossifies the economy and diminishes its responsiveness to changes in market data, especially those that take place in sectors whose primary goals are unrelated to the objectives pursued by politically influential agents. It bears mentioning here that such changes are bound to be particularly rapid and numerous in a globalized economy, as international markets are necessarily "anarchic" (i.e., not subject to any single political authority) on account of spanning multiple jurisdictions (Leeson, 2007). Hence, attempting to address global economic challenges by means of implementing inherently local and inward-looking industrial policies appears to be a self-defeating proposition.

Relatedly, employees who work for the aforementioned politically privileged businesses are likely to be lulled into a false sense of security – they might become convinced of having permanently escaped the vagaries of the global market by entering a perpetual alliance with local power structures. However, the belief that the political realm offers protection from job instability is a misconception. After all, just as the market domain is the field of entrepreneurial competition for customer attention, the political domain is the field of interest group competition for coercive control over society, with "elite" representatives of such interest groups wielding primary influence over voter preferences (Holcombe, 2021).

Moreover, one should bear in mind that, other things being equal, the direction of regime policy is more unpredictable and chaotic than the direction of market trends, as the latter are normally disciplined by the profit and loss criterion and reliant on the predictive power of the price system, while the former is subject to the largely arbitrary whims of power-hungry cliques (Inkina, 2019). Thus, seeking employment stability by becoming professionally involved in the implementation of an industrial policy might be a particularly risky move, especially in a global economy where dynamic entrepreneurialism exerts constant pressure on the feasibility of politically driven grand projects. That is to say, wishing to circumvent the challenge of forging a protean career by seeking the cushy comforts of bureaucratic policymaking may ultimately backfire by recreating this very challenge in an exceptionally dramatic form, characteristic of those cases where purposely reactive rule followers are suddenly thrust into the middle of a competitive market as a result of a major political shakeup.

Finally, one cannot overlook the fact that industrial policies are typically advocated by those who perceive international relations as an inexorably antagonistic zero-sum game. Consequently, they not only support the governmental cartelization of technological development but also attempt to eliminate the positive externalities associated with international technological diffusion, seeing their existence as a major incentive for economic espionage (D'Elia, 2018; Li and Alon, 2020). By the same token, they hinder the emergence of prosumer networks capable of generating further positive externalities in the form of bottom-up innovations shared on an open-source basis. In other words, by creating an adversarial atmosphere of mutual mistrust and research secrecy, advocates of industrial policies discourage proactivity on the part of innovative tinkerers deprived of access to products ready for reverse engineering.

In sum, waging trade wars, implementing national industrial plans, and pursuing similar economically isolationist and politically adversarial measures hamper the development of the proactive society on multiple fronts. However, as soon as one realizes that analogous measures aimed at promoting alleged self-determination are sometimes prescribed with respect to individuals, not just nations, further institutional impediments to proactivity enter the picture.

Perhaps the most popular among the recently raised proposals of this kind is the introduction of so-called guaranteed basic income (Howard, 2024). Just as the declared aim of implementing an industrial policy is to ensure a given country's self-determination by making it independent of foreign imports, the declared aim of introducing unconditional basic income (hereafter UBI) is to ensure every individual's self-determination by making everyone's baseline earnings independent of having gainful employment. Thus, in both cases, the ultimate goal is to sever a given entity's livelihood security from its willingness to engage in value creation within the ambit of large-scale social cooperation.

Among the most frequently invoked justifications for UBI is the claim that it can mitigate the perils of permanent technological unemployment brought about by the advent of "intelligent" automation (Hughes, 2014). In other words, it is, for all practical purposes, yet another incarnation of the centuries-old Luddite fear that sufficiently advanced machine labor can enduringly displace the vast majority of human labor. As such fears necessarily portray human labor and machine labor as substitutes rather than complements, they conspicuously overlook the unique human trait of proactivity and implicitly discourage tapping into its potential, both on the personal and the organizational levels.

However, as machines, just like all other tools – including those capable of big-data-driven "self-optimization" – are by their very nature purely reactive, they by definition cannot replace the human capacity for proactive problem identification and innovative solution design. Even more importantly, they are unable to do so even with regard to low-skill-requiring jobs, provided that performing the latter well demands at least a modicum of sound interpersonal skills such as active listening, non-verbal communication, empathy, and social imagination, the common denominator of which is proactive relationship building (Thompson, 2005).

Hence, as neo-Luddite-style calls for UBI misleadingly identify technological capital, not human capital, as the "ultimate resource" (Simon, 1996) responsible for continued socioeconomic growth and development, they are counterproductive insofar as they discourage the very proactivity that is indispensable for using technological advancements in the most value-creative manner. And given the degree to which such calls can generate self-fulfilling prophecies driven by defeatism and learned helplessness, their influence on the prospects for the emergence of an authentically proactive society can be particularly harmful.

Next, it should be kept in mind that as technological complexity increases and necessitates the establishment of ever more fine-grained organizational structures, even nonexecutive employees can be progressively expected to display entrepreneurial orientation (Miron and Hudson, 2014). In other words, the introduction of innovative methods of automating routine processes and forecasting repetitive events enlarges the importance of the proactive ability to sift out unusual processes and extraordinary events, whose neglect is bound to derail even the most supposedly foolproof "intelligent" systems. For example, even the most sophisticated credit rating algorithm will make bad decisions if it is not supervised by prudent specialists capable of seeing through the fraudulent nature of certain allegedly safe financial instruments posted as collaterals, such as, say, triple-A-rated mortgage-backed securities based on subprime loans.

In addition, technological innovations can themselves give rise to new kinds of human experience, which have to be proactively accommodated by competent proxy-entrepreneurs in order to ensure customer satisfaction. For instance, designers of driverless car interfaces should aim at automating lower-level tasks such as navigation while allowing drivers to focus more deeply on higher-level tasks such as creating a unique set of memorable destinations for their passengers (Brown and Osborn, 2019). That is to say, in a world increasingly capable of automating the mundane, they should become all the more adept at enhancing the potential of human agency to craft personal experiences and delight in the special character of volitional behavior.

The above observations serve as telling indicators of the fact that, contrary to the neo-Luddite proponents of UBI, the advent of "intelligent" algorithms further elevates the role of human input instead of diminishing it. Thus, the mindset according to which human agents should have no qualms about receding from the picture as algorithmic systems become more sophisticated and pervasive is particularly antithetical to the promotion of proxy-entrepreneurship and other forms of value-creative employee initiative. This is because it ultimately encourages people to content themselves with the status of idle consumers of the supposedly unconditionally distributed plenty generated by hypothetical hyper-productive machines, which is the epitome of mindless stagnation.

Finally, the preceding remarks imply that in the age of widespread automation, permanent learning rather than permanent resting on one's laurels is likely to be the default mode of professional orientation. More specifically, one might suggest in this context that while in the managerial society, employees typically evaluate their earnings prospects in terms of their possession of specialized technical skills, in the proactive society, it is their value productivity – understood as their direct ability to provide consumer satisfaction and obtain the corresponding remuneration – that is likely to serve as the primary benchmark of occupational performance. This follows naturally from the fact that as routine managerial tasks are steadily taken over by sufficiently advanced machines, the capability to organize their labor in the most consumer-responsive manner becomes far more important than the capability to replicate their purely technical achievements.

That is to say, in the proactive society, it is not knowledge per se that provides one with a competitive advantage in the labor market – all the hackneyed statements about the arrival of the "knowledge economy" notwithstanding – but rather the (proxy-)entrepreneurial acumen necessary to allocate knowledge-intensive factors of production to their most value-productive uses (Bylund, 2025). This, in turn, suggests that in a highly automated work environment, job descriptions can be expected to become increasingly protean – defined primarily in terms not of the specialized procedures that one is to carry out, but in terms of the rapidly and uniquely changeable market settings in which one is to pursue the ever-receding horizon of perfect customer satisfaction.

Thus, we reach the somewhat ironic conclusion that the world of technological plenty envisioned by UBI proponents can possibly come into existence only in a socioeconomic atmosphere in which people are inherently opposed to the prospect of being paid independent of their productivity, seen as a particularly potent disincentive to proxy-entrepreneurial initiative in the face of protean workplace volatility. In other words, it might well be the case that the very phenomena that make UBI feasible also make it undesirable, which might be regarded as an additional argument for its practical economic unattainability (Iglesias and Block, 2019).

In sum, the greatest economic obstacle to the emergence of a full-blooded proactive society consists in the implementation of various policies grounded in the belief that the unprecedented wealth created in the transitional phase between the managerial society and the semi-proactive society can allow humankind to scale back on global cooperation, slip back into a mostly reactive mode, and freely pursue the goals of regional economic independence and unconditional personal comfort for everyone, including the voluntarily nonproductive.

As, however, the ultimate driving force behind such policies is the active support of society or at least its passive assent, highlighting their economic counterproductivity and their unique capacity to deplete the potential of nascent proactivity is not enough to ensure their curtailment, let alone their outright abandonment. To make this a feasible outcome, the broader impact of the relevant social attitudes, beliefs, and orientations needs to be explored in greater detail. Subsequently, some actionable revisions of these attitudes have to be suggested. It is to such considerations that I wish to turn in the following section.

3.2 Social challenges to the proactive society

There are at least two widespread social tendencies present in the socioeconomic environment, characteristic of today's developed countries that appear to be especially potent in inhibiting the promise of mature proactivity. The first of these is rooted in the conviction that specialization, division of labor, technological advancement, and similar phenomena, together with their lifestyle ramifications such as urbanization, occupational digitalization, and the increase in remote work, progressively liberate workers from the necessity of interacting with "traditional" social structures and institutions (Preece, 2021), allowing them either to self-select into strictly like-minded groups or to retreat comfortably into personal bubbles of asociality.

The second of the abovementioned tendencies, on the other hand, is grounded in the opposition to the social atomization and anonymization supposedly driven by the excesses of specialization, division of labor, technological dependence, global interrelatedness, and rootless urbanism (Lundestad, 2004). In order to counter these developments, their opponents typically propose measures such as the promotion of local economic self-reliance, reshoring, subsidizing vocational training, and encouraging staunchly patriotic sentiments, believing that greater social cohesion is bound to result in greater economic well-being even in the absence of some key benefits of globalization.

The main danger associated with the former orientation consists in the fact that there might be an inverse relationship between the degree of the division of labor and the quality of the informal institutions needed to sustain interpersonal trust and other coordinative prerequisites of complex social cooperation (Davis, 2006). Thus, it might turn out that far from being able to retreat into voluntary ghettoes of cultural and ideological self-segregation, employees in a highly specialized, transnational economy need to be even more prosocially inclined than their counterparts from less developed and more isolated economies. In other words, maintaining the productivity characteristic of technologically advanced and functionally differentiated labor requires an exceptionally pronounced level of proactive engagement, which is necessary for preserving shared visions of professional accomplishment and which, incidentally, provides yet another telling illustration of the truth that the role of human capital (and, in this context, particularly the role of bridging capital) cannot be automated away.

On the other hand, the chief difficulty related to the latter orientation stems from the mistaken belief that a society sufficiently equipped with high-quality bonding capital and a robust set of soft institutions can achieve steadily growing wealth while, or even through, implementing heavy tariffs, severe immigration restrictions, and other policies constitutive of socioeconomic isolationism. Given the fact that the division of labor is limited by the extent of the market and that entrepreneurial human capital is the "ultimate resource" behind persistent economic development and improving social well-being, the assumption that reducing one's dependence on the global market is the road to new highs of national prosperity is misplaced, to say the least (Kennan 2013; Contractor, 2025). Furthermore, the negative consequences of pursuing national economic self-sufficiency are likely to be particularly painful if a given country is a recent beneficiary of globalization, as they can be expected to involve a rapid deterioration of the capital stock accumulated during the preceding period of unobstructed transborder cooperation.

In sum, the first of the tendencies under consideration assumes that, as far as wealth generation is concerned, sufficiently rapid globalization can eliminate the need for social cohesion, while the second suggests that a sufficient degree of social cohesion can eliminate the need for globalization. And yet, as the maintenance of intricate global collaboration requires the presence of strong informal institutions, and as an accelerated economic retrogression associated with abandoning the advantages of globalization is likely to bring about increased social tensions, both orientations in question can be justifiably seen as counterproductive and self-defeating.

Their fatal common denominator appears to be the neglect of the entrepreneurial potential of human nature, which, in this context, invites the kind of proactive engagement that allows for using one's specialized professional skills as the supporting beams of one's broader community, thereby converting one's individual capital into social capital and for using one's strong communal ties as springboards for intercommunal exchange, thereby converting one's bonding capital into bridging capital.

More specifically, the defects of both of those tendencies can be avoided, while their respective merits can be preserved, if their proponents decide to make a conscious use of the catallactic potential of socioeconomic activity, bearing in mind the whole range of meanings embedded in the terms "catallactics" and "catallaxy", whose root verb can be rendered not only as "to exchange" but also as "to admit in the community" and "to change from enemy into friend" (Hayek, 1976: 108–109). Thus, safeguarding the cooperative achievements of the managerial society in its global form, let alone unleashing the productive potential of its proactive counterpart, may well require imbuing one's professional discipline with the aura of neighborly conviviality and treating prospective foreign business partners as members of an extended family of enterprising humans.

Such undertakings may be regarded as conscious efforts at elevating the "extended order of human cooperation" (Hayek, 1989: 6) to a qualitatively higher level so as to prevent its possible breakdown caused either by an excessive magnitude of cosmopolitan fragmentation or by a large-scale defensive retreat into tribal ghettoization or by some combination of both. As such, they might be defined as catallactic activities in the deepest sense of this term, focused on creating bridges between narrowly understood commercial mutuality and broadly conceived social coherence.

At this point, one could object by pointing out that the extended order is by definition a spontaneous phenomenon, whose very survival, let alone flourishing, is predicated on not trying to tweak it or push it in a particular direction by means of intentional reorientation. Such an objection, however, would be based on a faulty assumption. Admittedly, certain important manifestations of the extended order, such as market price signals, invisible-hand-driven harmonies of interests, and positive externalities brought about by technological diffusion, can perform their beneficial functions even if no one consciously strives to ensure their continued and reliable operation, or even if hardly anyone understands their full logical nature and the attendant economic significance. And yet, even though the extended order is clearly a spontaneous phenomenon on the macro level, it is also obviously a designed and deliberate system on the micro level, as its shape derives from an endless stream of purposive interactions between volitional individuals.

In other words, the emergence of bottom-up, "socially evolutionary" institutional patterns contains an essential, microlevel element of "social rationalism" (Salerno, 1990), whereby various intentionally thought-out ideas dovetail or clash, leading to the ascendancy or decline of distinct intellectual traditions and their broader cultural ramifications. In view of this, it appears only natural that in a socioeconomic milieu whose continued existence, let alone further development, depends crucially on widespread understanding of abstract and relatively complex concepts such as comparative advantage, network externalities, and opportunity costs, proactive attempts at influencing the direction of intellectual and cultural drift are bound to become increasingly consequential. This, one should note, has nothing whatsoever in common with trying to resurrect visions of centrally planned utopias and comprehensive schemes of social engineering, but, on the contrary, it indicates the indispensability of grasping how spontaneous proactivity drives the orderly functioning of intricate international cooperation.

Another false dichotomy into which the inhabitants of today's developed world can easily fall is centered on the role of hierarchy in social organization. Those who put much trust in the "emancipatory" potential of technology, remote work, and high-skill freelancing might be inclined to believe that all kinds of hierarchies, including professional chains of command, are destined to wither away in a sufficiently dynamic and innovative economy. On the other hand, individuals concerned about the dissolution of robust soft institutions in a globalized environment might be willing to conclude that only interventionist national policies, and thus greater empowerment of coercive bureaucratic hierarchies, can safeguard such institutions and ensure their effective operation.

While the former view errs in assuming that proactivity is necessarily antithetical to hierarchization, the latter wrongly implies that the epitome of proactive social engagement is comprehensive political regimentation. With respect to the first error, one needs to realize that owners, executives, and other boss figures perform the essential function of setting up and enforcing the "rules of the game" needed to coordinate multiple specialized tasks. Such coordination, one should add, is particularly vital whenever major strategic decisions have to be made urgently, critical macro-scale knowledge is concentrated on the topmost organizational level, and a substantial degree of interdepartmental or interindustry harmonization is necessary (Foss and Klein, 2022).

Similar situations are likely to become increasingly frequent in the proactive society, given its characteristic features such as the salient presence of dynamic transaction costs, pervasive technological innovation, and an exceptional abundance of separate business entities. Thus, well-designed hierarchical structures can be plausibly argued to be not just non-hostile to the exercise of proactivity, but actually crucial in stimulating it. After all, a proxy-entrepreneur can make profitable use of his extensive discretionary powers only if he knows perfectly well what the precise scope of these powers is – otherwise, he is bound to encroach upon the professional domains of his fellow proxy-entrepreneurs, non-entrepreneurial employees, and full-scale owner-entrepreneurs (Foss, Foss, and Klein, 2007). And it is precisely the role of hierarchical management to specify in unambiguous terms what the executive purview of all those respective professional groups is.

That being said, proactivity-stimulating hierarchies can fulfill their potential only if their members are intrinsically motivated to subordinate themselves to the overarching goals of such stratified systems (Karimi, Malek, and Farani, 2022). This, in turn, implies that, as mentioned in the earlier part of this section, intricately organized occupational structures of this kind cannot operate effectively in the absence of deep trust, sincere mutual respect, communal conviviality, and other forms of robust social capital rooted in resilient informal institutions.

This contention leads us to the latter horn of the abovementioned dichotomy, that is, to the view that protecting social vibrancy against the supposed ravages of rootless globalism requires empowering political and bureaucratic hierarchies to implement extensive national programs consisting of elements such as pronatalist incentives, "civic education", and obligatory community service.

The primary problem with this approach is the assumption that high-quality bonding capital can be administratively manufactured instead of having to emerge in a spontaneous manner over a long period of time, gradually coalescing as a result of innumerable sociable acts undertaken by cooperatively minded individuals. Understanding the nature and role of proactivity in fostering reliable and far-reaching social collaboration makes the problematic character of this assumption particularly visible, as it highlights the extent to which entrepreneurial freedom and communal intimacy are ultimately two sides of the same coin.

For instance, as indicated earlier, deep-seated relations of genuine trust can be established only on the basis of voluntary contacts characterized by respect for the autonomy of all participating parties in making use of their respective contextual knowledge (Ikeda, 2002). As can be easily noticed, such respect is the common denominator of both familial and commercial interactions, while being conspicuously absent from interactions aiming at the imposition of broad-brush national policies, where coercive uniformization and the attendant insensitivity to individual circumstances are practically a prerequisite. In other words, hard paternalism is the very opposite of trusting in the rationality of ordinary members of society and their spontaneous groupings, and as such it appears to be a singularly inappropriate tool for fostering the development of robust social capital.

Moreover, even if the members of a given community were to be favorably disposed toward the prospect of being paternalistically regimented by their political leaders, putting the utmost trust in their grandiose social schemes, they would by the same token deprive themselves of the ability to make free use of the tacit dimension of their knowledge (Duguid, 2005). This, in turn, would subject them to an "active" form of learned helplessness, whereby they not so much remain inert in the face of looming problems, but undertake only those kinds of supposed solutions to them that are administratively designed and imposed in a one-fits-all manner from above. In other words, adopting such an attitude would stunt their individual problem-solving capacities grounded in their contextual understanding and inarticulable practical wisdom, thus leading to the very opposite of genuine social vibrancy and deep-rooted communal resilience.

Finally, one should note that even in the realm of conflict resolution – that is, in the realm that is typically seen as naturally falling under the jurisdiction of coercive territorial monopolies – maintaining authentic social cohesion normally requires a substantial degree of bottom-up initiative related to the informal settlement of disputes. Especially in a dynamic world of rapid cultural shifts, ubiquitous technological novelties, and frequent international interactions, social entrepreneurs need to be actively involved in discovering new combinations of social capital that are particularly likely to foster harmonious communal cooperation (Chamlee-Wright, 2008). That is to say, even on the seemingly quintessentially political level of social organization, the existence of robust trust-building institutions may be antithetical to the pursuit of overarching national policies.

In sum, the two major social tendencies discussed in the present section are at odds with the flourishing of proactivity not in virtue of opposing it directly, but rather on account of misplacing its focal point and its scope of influence. The view according to which urbanization, globalization, digitalization, and similar phenomena can increase individual productivity by doing away with traditions, hierarchies, and unwanted social interactions wrongly suggests that the primary locus of proactivity is personal, not interpersonal. On the other hand, the view according to which globalization is uniquely capable of damaging the crucial institutions responsible for preserving social coherence mistakenly assumes that proactivity has to emanate from some sort of paternalistic command center instead of being nurtured though horizontal and spontaneous networks.

Whether these twin errors can be successfully avoided is ultimately a function of the extent to which society at large can see through the avalanche of simplistic bromides that falsify the relationship between proactive behavior and communal solidity. This task is all the more challenging in today's day and age, when familiarizing oneself with various ideas is admittedly easy in view of their near-universal accessibility, but their genuine understanding is significantly difficult on account of their ubiquitous misrepresentations and caricatures present in mass media. Thus, an essential prerequisite of accomplishing the socioeconomic goal of unleashing the full potential of widespread proactivity consists in accomplishing the cognitive goal of exercising a sufficient degree of meta-proactivity, that is, personal intellectual initiative aimed at grasping the proper nature of the concept in question. In the following section, I shall explore at greater length the character of this latter challenge.

3.3 Cognitive challenges to the proactive society

As I indicated in the concluding paragraph of the previous section, tapping into the productive power of the proactive orientation requires firm intellectual and informational foundations. Acquiring those appears to be of particular importance in the so-called information society, where the value of critical engagement with the propositional content received from the outside world is exceptionally vital. The same goes for the so-called connectivity economy, where knowing when to remain disconnected from a given stream of data is as essential, if not more so, than knowing when to seek connection with any such data source.

If proactivity is to be defined as, among other things, the ability to act of one's own accord in anticipation of unique future contingencies, meta-proactivity can be defined as the corresponding ability to evaluate critically the conceptual resources at one's disposal that can potentially be used to address such contingencies. This implies that the most fatally reactive approach that one can adopt in the "information economy" is not to persist in willful ignorance, but to absorb completely passively whatever packages of data are hurled in one's direction, believing them to be ready-made answers to whatever problems one is confronted with. In other words, while the advent and maturation of the information revolution generated substantial productivity gains in virtue of, for example, reducing transaction costs, creating positive network externalities, aiding product differentiation, and accelerating technological diffusion (Varian, Farrell, and Shapiro, 2004), they have also, by the same token, raised the qualitative bar for capturing those gains.

This contention can be illustrated on the basis of a number of illustrations related to several distinct roles that one usually performs as a member of society. For instance, a consumer who exercises his purchasing choices in the information economy has a multitude of potentially useful aids at his fingertips, including brand guides, quality certificates, consumer reports, review platforms, etc., all neatly assembled and readily accessible online (DiLorenzo, 2011). However, such an abundance of possibly relevant information in no way diminishes the problem of converting it into actionable knowledge, as the consumer under consideration must still personally evaluate the trustworthiness and timeliness of the sources at his disposal. Here is where meta-proactivity comes into the picture, allowing for an individual selection of particular data channels based on a subjective reconstruction of the motives of those channels' operators and a qualitative assessment of their overall professionalism. Without exercising it, the aids mentioned above, far from assisting customers in making prudent, utility-enhancing decisions, are more likely to disorient them and make them particularly susceptible to offers of a flashy and manipulative nature, thus ultimately decreasing the level of their cognitive preparation.

Similarly, investors and speculators who seek profitable financial instruments in the information economy can make use of a plethora of convenient tools such as free stock scanners, free analyses provided by reputable financial institutions, hedge fund trackers, and earnings calendars. However, the widespread accessibility and facile usability of these tools are the reason why by themselves they offer no investment edge to any of their users. On the contrary, their sheer number can easily overwhelm the purely reactive user, who is willing to treat them as a shortcut to wealth rather than at best a baseline in need of detailed personal refinement. As a matter of fact, the very existence of such informational accessories makes generating sustained above-average returns all the more difficult, as it immediately eliminates the advantage associated with solving the relatively simple task of collecting and assembling relevant public data, the only profitable advantage remaining being a superior ability to appraise specific bundles of business assets in view of uncertain configurations of future prices (Herbener and Rapp, 2016).

Finally, voters interested in making maximally prudent electoral choices in the information society may resort to an abundance of freely available political analyses, opinion polls, prediction markets, in-depth psychological profiles of particular candidates, etc. And yet, as in the previous two cases, such tools are bound to remain useless or even counterproductive if their users cannot independently assess their reliability and respectability. More specifically, for instance, a particular opinion poll may be misleading insofar as it tends to underestimate those voter groups that are traditionally reluctant to disclose their electoral preferences. Similarly, a specific prediction market may be too broadly focused to offer credible forecasts concerning the outcomes of sufficiently local events. Such considerations – together with the attendant ability to use the relevant tools in appropriate combinations (Dana, Atanasov, Tetlock, and Mellers, 2019) – have to be deeply understood and thoroughly internalized in one's personal decision-making process if it is to result in genuinely informed choices, and this is precisely the area in which meta-proactivity can shield the voter from rational ignorance, rational irrationality, political self-delusion, and similar epistemic obstacles.

All that being said, however, one should bear in mind that the cognitive potential and temporal capacity of even the most fortunately endowed and diligently prepared human being are necessarily limited. In other words, even a veritable genius equipped with iron-clad discipline and an abundance of psychological experience is incapable of conducting an exhaustive analysis of all possibly relevant data sources, let alone of every piece of information emanating from them. Thus, an essential element of dealing with the challenge of informational selection and evaluation in the proactive society consists in developing the instantaneous ability to block off intrusive sources of informational noise and sludge.

One notable way of accomplishing this goal appears to be grounded primarily in the capability to choose carefully one's personal "circle of competence" (Eraut, 1998) and stay strictly within its confines whenever it is possible. By doing so, one should be able to minimize the chance of coming into contact with the kind of information that one is unable to assess with a sufficient degree of confidence, thereby making sure not to incur inordinate risks and not to overtax one's cognitive resources.

However, retreating into an adequately narrow circle of competence is challenging in proportion to how politically centralized and regimented the available places of residence are, especially those in the nearest vicinity to one's native habitat, that is, those that are likely to be particularly easy to acclimatize in. More specifically, the more one is subject to unwanted external intrusions orchestrated by the use of political (i.e., institutionally coercive) means, the more one has to widen one's circle of competence against one's will. For instance, if one happens to live in a world of fiat (i.e., politically controlled) money, then one's acts of monetary calculation need to take into consideration not only one's expected earnings and expenses but also the extent to which an expansionary monetary policy of a given political regime is likely to diminish the purchasing power of the local legal tender. Similarly, if one happens to live in a coercively paternalistic system, then in executing one's entrepreneurial projects, one needs to forecast accurately not only the actual wants of one's prospective customers but also the shape of future policies aimed at restricting their autonomous choices.

Needless to say, the problem in question becomes especially acute as political regimes undergo the process of overt or covert international integration and the attendant fiscal, monetary, and regulatory harmonization (Hülsmann, 1997). To phrase the issue in slightly different terms, if constitutional protections can be construed as guarantors of the inviolability of the individual's private space, and insofar as institutional competition can be regarded as the most effective method of enforcing such protections (Long, 2008), the diminution of such competition is bound to make individual private spaces increasingly unsafe, thus necessitating the corresponding expansions of individual circles of competence.

This indicates that another vital form of meta-proactivity in the information society might consist in undertaking successful ventures in the field of institutional entrepreneurship aimed at setting up authentically independent pockets of contractual governance. Insofar as such communal associations can be governed in a genuinely participatory manner and engender robust relations of trust, their inhabitants can enjoy legal stability, organizational predictability, cultural intimacy, and commercial transparency. Consequently, they can keep their personal circles of competence manageably narrow, focusing their cognitive resources on the qualitative filtration of those kinds of information that correspond to their distinctive concerns, interests, duties, and values.

Furthermore, "shopping around" in order to find a self-governing community of this kind that is particularly in tune with one's preferences is likely to yield highly credible insights. This is because such communities are bound to be relatively small in size (Randma-Liiv and Sarapuu, 2025), which, in combination with their participatory, trust-based character, minimizes the likelihood of their reputation being systematically and lastingly misrepresented, either in support by their allies or in opposition by their enemies.

In addition, even in the worst-case scenario of any such organizational entity becoming dysfunctional to the point of dissolution, its largely self-contained character and lack of expansionist ambitions prevent such an event from generating cascading negative externalities capable of threatening the stability of a wider network of similar institutional microsystems. On the contrary, such an occurrence might actually provide valuable lessons to institutional entrepreneurs eager to improve the resilience of their ventures, as well as to the inhabitants of the dissolved community willing either to participate in its recreation or to migrate quickly to a more promising habitat. This observation not only underscores the "anti-fragile" (Taleb, 2012) nature of decentralized, multipolar, and contractual sociopolitical systems but also emphasizes the fact that "anti-fragility" has an important cognitive dimension, whose appreciation appears particularly urgent in the information society. Unsurprisingly, it also ties in naturally with the remarks concerning the cognitive characteristics of the proactive society made in Section 1.6.

It is also worth mentioning that in the era of proxy-entrepreneurship, protean careers, prosumer creativity, and other phenomena associated with the increasingly salient role of proactivity in business settings, cognitive anti-fragility is as essential on the personal level as it is on the social level. That is to say, in a globalized world of constant confrontations with anonymous, impersonal sources of highly specialized and multidisciplinary information, it is ultimately impossible to avoid making at least occasional mistakes. This is especially so in the early stage of discovering one's circle of competence, when resorting to the trial-and-error method is indispensable (Bridge, 2021). Thus, instead of trying to accomplish the impossible goal of steering clear of every conceivable mistake, a meta-proactive agent should strive to identify those mistakes that are affordable and likely to generate valuable developmental feedback.

The above reflections drive home the extent to which the phenomenon of proactivity overlaps with the concept of entrepreneurship broadly conceived – that is, the notion that all human action is ineradicably speculative and experientially adaptive. By the same token, they also imply that establishing one's unique circle of competence in the information society may require consciously going against the grain of received procedural wisdom in a quasi-Schumpeterian manner. For instance, one might reasonably conclude that the majority of chatbots are unreliable substitutes for search engines insofar as, in virtue of being fed copious amounts of low-quality "big data", they are far more prone to being governed by the principle of "garbage in, garbage out" (Hanson et al., 2023). Consequently, in order not to be misled by their informational output, a meta-proactive agent might be inclined to devise his personal set of heuristic rules used to filter away what he regards as the most common and potentially distortive failings of such AI tools. Alternatively, he might spurn their use altogether and stick with traditional search engines until the moment when, in his estimation, the failings in question have been rectified successfully.

In a similar vein, such an individual might decide to reduce his reliance on impersonal, virtually delivered information to a minimum and put extra effort into building a local cognitive network of robust social capital. Exhibiting such a pronounced preference for "traditional" methods of collecting valuable insights might, once again, be counted as an example of a quasi-entrepreneurial rebellion against mainstream tendencies. And, given the qualitative premium associated with relying primarily on information gathered from trusted, thoroughly vetted, and consistently unfailing sources, a "revolt" of this kind may well give its pursuer a substantial cognitive edge (Zimmer and Henry, 2017).

In sum, the ultimate, overarching cognitive challenge to the emergence of a mature proactive society consists in rejecting firmly the notion that there is such a thing as a free informational lunch. In other words, it entails the realization that an abundance of data and free tools for processing does not by itself contribute to the alleviation of the problem of scarcity.

As I have pointed out several times in previous chapters, scarcity is a moving target, whose pursuit leads to the steady replacement of quantitative goals with their qualitative counterparts and to the diminishing value of instruments coupled with the increasing value of the competencies required of their users. Thus, any inhabitant of the information society who wishes to use its distinct epistemic characteristics to his advantage needs to adopt a cognitive perspective that draws upon various entrepreneurial ideal types. That is to say, he needs to display, among other things, Schumpeterian "creative destruction" in the form of questioning the potential groupthink easily perpetuated by chatbots and similar AI services, Kirznerian alertness to overlooked and undervalued bits of knowledge, and the ability to pierce the veil of Knightian uncertainty through making reliable projections of future configurations of the relevant data.

All in all, then, far from treating various technological accoutrements as partial or complete substitutes of their intellectual faculties, (meta-)proactive individuals need to treat them as subordinate complements at best, which have to be consciously adapted to particular personal skillsets and roadmaps in order to become truly useful. This, in turn, suggests that perhaps the single most defining feature of the proactive society is the emphasis it puts on self-starting individualism, that is, individualism conceived in terms not of psychological selfishness or functional self-sufficiency, but of self-directed and unique integration into a complex system of social cooperation grounded in advanced specialization, fine-grained division of labor, and continuous innovation.

Insofar as this observation can serve not only as the upshot of the present section but also as the summation of the considerations investigated in the whole of the current book, let us use it as a natural segway into its concluding part.

Bibliography

Baumol, W. J., 1990. Entrepreneurship: Productive, unproductive, and destructive. Journal of Political Economy 98 (5), 893–921.

Bridge, S., 2021. Facing uncertainty: An entrepreneurial view of the future? Journal of Management & Organization 27 (2), 312–323.

Brown, E. S., Osborn, K., 2019. The human agency driverless cars must preserve. Ethnographic Praxis in Industry Conference Proceedings, 159–169.

Bylund, P. L., 2025. Entrepreneurship and Evolutionary Economics. Cambridge University Press.

Chamlee-Wright, E., 2008. The structure of social capital: An Austrian perspective on its nature and development. Review of Political Economy 20 (1), 41–58.

Chen, Y., Zhang, S., Miao, J., 2023. The negative effects of the US-China trade war on innovation: Evidence from the Chinese ICT industry. Technovation 123, Article 102734.

Contractor, F. J., 2025. Assessing the economic impact of tariffs: Adaptations by multinationals and traders to mitigate tariffs. Review of International Business and Strategy 35 (2–3), 190–213.

Dana, J., Atanasov, P., Tetlock, P., Mellers, B., 2019. Are markets more accurate than polls? The surprising informational value of "just asking". Judgment and Decision Making 14 (2), 135–147.

Davis, L. S., 2006. Growing apart: The division of labor and the breakdown of informal institutions. Journal of Comparative Economics 34 (1), 75–91.

D'Elia, D., 2018. Industrial policy: The holy grail of French cybersecurity strategy? Journal of Cyber Policy 3 (3), 385–406.

DiLorenzo, T. J., 1984. The political economy of national industrial policy. Cato Journal 4 (2), 587–607.

DiLorenzo, T. J., 2011. A note on the Canard of "asymmetric information" as a source of market failure. Quarterly Journal of Austrian Economics 14 (2), 249–255.

Duguid, P., 2005. "The art of knowing": Social and tacit dimensions of knowledge and the limits of the community of practice. The Information Society 21 (2), 109–118.

Elert, N., Stenkula, M., 2022. Intrapreneurship: Productive and non-productive. Entrepreneurship Theory and Practice 46 (5), 1423–1439.

Eraut, M., 1998. Concepts of competence. Journal of Interprofessional Care 12 (2), 127–139.
Foss, N. J., Klein, P. G., 2022. Why Managers Matter: The Perils of the Bossless Company. Hachette, UK.
Foss, K., Foss, N. J., Klein, P. G., 2007. Original and derived judgment: An entrepreneurial theory of economic organization. Organization Studies 28 (12), 1893–1912.
Friedman, J., Kraus, W., 2011. Engineering the Financial Crisis: Systemic Risk and the Failure of Regulation. University of Pennsylvania Press, Philadelphia, PA.
Grossman, G. M., Helpman, E., 2015. Globalization and growth. American Economic Review 105 (5), 100–104.
Hanson, B., Stall, S., Cutcher-Gershenfeld, J., Vrouwenvelder, K., Wirz, C., Rao, Y., Peng, G., 2023. Garbage in, garbage out: Mitigating risks and maximizing benefits of AI in research. Nature 623 (7985), 28–31.
Hayek, F. A., 1976. Law, Legislation and Liberty, Vol. 2: The Mirage of Social Justice. University of Chicago Press, Chicago, IL.
Hayek, F. A., 1989. The Fatal Conceit: The Errors of Socialism. University of Chicago Press, Chicago, IL.
Herbener, J., Rapp, D., 2016. Toward a subjective approach to investment appraisal in light of Austrian value theory. Quarterly Journal of Austrian Economics 19 (1), 3–28.
Holcombe, R. G., 2013. Crony capitalism: By-product of big government. The Independent Review 17 (4), 541–559.
Holcombe, R. G., 2021. Elite influence on general political preferences. Journal of Government and Economics 3 (3), 100021.
Howard, J. L., 2024. Guaranteed basic income from the perspective of self-determination theory. Journal of Management Studies.
Hughes, J., 2014. A strategic opening for a basic income guarantee in the global crisis being created by AI, robots, desktop manufacturing and biomedicine. Journal of Ethics and Emerging Technologies 24 (1), 45–61.
Hülsmann, J. G., 1997. Political unification: A generalized progression theorem. Journal of Libertarian Studies 13 (1), 81–96.
Iglesias, D., Block, W., 2019. Universal basic income: A critique. Romanian Economic and Business Review 14 (3), 7–18.
Ikeda, S., 2002. The role of "social capital" in the market process. Journal des Economistes et des Etudes Humaines 12 (2), 229–240.
Inkina, S., 2019. Bureaucratic reform and Russian transition: The puzzles of policy-making process. Palgrave Communications 5 (1), 1–15.
Karimi, S., Malek, F. A., Farani, A. Y., 2022. The relationship between proactive personality and employees' creativity: The mediating role of intrinsic motivation and creative self-efficacy. Economic Research-Ekonomska Istraživanja 35 (1), 4500–4519.
Kennan, J., 2013. Open borders. Review of Economic Dynamics 16 (2), L1–L13.
Khanna, G., Shih, K., Weinberger, A., Xu, M., Yu, M., 2023. Trade liberalization and Chinese students in US higher education. Review of Economics and Statistics, 1–46.

Leeson, P. T., 2007. Efficient anarchy. Public Choice 130 (1–2), 41–53.
Li, S., Alon, I., 2020. China's intellectual property rights provocation: A political economy view. Journal of International Business Policy 3 (1), 60–72.
Long, R. T., 2008. Market Anarchism as Constitutionalism. In: Long, R. T., Machan, T. R. (Eds.), Anarchism/Minarchism: Is a Government Part of a Free Country? Ashgate, Burlington, VT, 133–151.
Lundestad, G., 2004. Why does globalization encourage fragmentation? International Politics 41, 265–276.
Miron, W., Hudson, D., 2014. Enabling employee entrepreneurship in large technology firms. Technology Innovation Management Review 4 (2), 23–32.
Preece, J., 2021. Liberated work: Responding to the unshackling of 'work' from 'place'. Corporate Real Estate Journal 11 (2), 158–172.
Randma-Liiv, T., Sarapuu, K., 2025. Small states as poster children of robust governance? Small States & Territories 8 (1), 116–120.
Salerno, J. T., 1990. Ludwig von Mises as social rationalist. Review of Austrian Economics 4 (1), 26–54.
Simon, J. L., 1996. The Ultimate Resource 2. Princeton University Press.
Taleb, N., 2012. Antifragile: Things That Gain from Disorder. Random House, New York.
Thompson, J. A., 2005. Proactive personality and job performance: A Social Capital Perspective. Journal of Applied Psychology 90 (5), 1011–1017.
Tuncer, F. F., 2023. Discussing globalization and cultural hybridization. Universal Journal of History and Culture 5 (2), 85–103.
Varian, H. R., Farrell, J., Shapiro, C., 2004. The Economics of Information Technology: An Introduction. Cambridge University Press.
Weede, E., 2004. The diffusion of prosperity and peace by globalization. The Independent Review 9 (2), 165–186.
Zimmer, J. C., Henry, R. M., 2017. The role of social capital in selecting interpersonal information sources. Journal of the Association for Information Science and Technology 68 (1), 5–21.

Conclusion

While by now it is widely accepted that human capital constitutes the "ultimate resource" responsible for sustained socioeconomic growth and development, reflecting on the nature of the proactive society that drives home the still insufficiently appreciated fact that individual human initiative is the ultimate motive force that allows for unlocking this resource's latent potential. In this sense, engaging in the reflection under consideration can be seen as the culmination of the theory of economic growth and development grounded in the investigation of consecutive periods of economic history.

The agrarian society, one might argue, was organized around the belief in the primacy of land among the main factors of production. Thus, as land by itself, that is, in the absence of innovative thinking about its potential uses, is hardly modifiable in terms of its value productivity, the agrarian model was rather static and consequently unconducive to mature analysis of the sources and processes of wealth generation. The industrial society, with its conviction of the primacy of capital, stimulated numerous insightful observations regarding the prerequisites of creating enduring prosperity, but those observations were ultimately disappointingly misdirected toward the material side of production to the detriment of understanding the crucial role of the underlying volitional phenomena. Finally, the managerial society, with its faith in the primacy of finely divided and neatly regimented labor, not only provoked many perceptive insights into the nature of organizational effectiveness, but it was also needlessly marred by the vision of the economy as strictly divided into a minority of active decision-makers and a majority of reactive decision takers.

The proactive society, on the other hand, in contrast to all of its historical predecessors, cannot be meaningfully described as placing predominant emphasis on any single factor of production from the classical triad. Moreover, its character cannot be encapsulated simply by extending the triad in question through supplementing it with entrepreneurship treated as the overarching "fourth factor", as even then the analysis of its productive capacity remains sorely limited. Instead, its sufficiently thorough description has to rely on a significantly broader conception of creative agency capable of

DOI: 10.4324/9781003764557-5

unlocking the value present in previously unknown factor combinations, including those made or co-made by non-residual claimants. This conception, as I have attempted to argue in the present work, is precisely proactivity in its manifold manifestations such as self-startingness, proxy-entrepreneurship, protean career building, effectual self-discovery, consumer activism, and prosumer innovativeness.

Another historically oriented perspective on the road to the proactive society might be centered not on the primacy of various factors of production in various economic eras, but on the most important characteristics expected of a successful economic agent in each of those eras.

In the broadly conceived preindustrial era, agricultural householders, artisanal manufacturers, and feudal landowners alike were required to be considerably versatile and self-sufficient, skilled in a range of disparate disciplines and capable, if need be, of surviving on their own. This kind of versatility and self-sufficiency, however, was possible only in a world of relatively predictable consumer tastes, unchanging technological capabilities, and stable cultural patterns. Thus, in spite of the impressive range of useful traits exhibited by its most accomplished representatives, the preindustrial era was not particularly conducive to the full realization of the productive potential of human agency.

The industrial era, with its veritable explosion of labor-saving and quality-enhancing innovations, as well as the attendant social upheavals, was a period of considerably greater dynamism than its predecessor. By the same token, it was much more favorable to the display of mature entrepreneurial skills by ambitious and daring businesspeople. However, the degree of division of labor and organizational micromanagement that was necessitated by the transition to the industrial mode of production made the exercise of full-blooded entrepreneurialism at that time the domain of a comparatively small part of society.

In contrast, the technological, social, cultural, and economic developments of the recent years, analyzed in the consecutive chapters of the present work, demand an increasing reliance on solutions such as worker empowerment, managerial delayering, intrapreneurship, lifelong learning, peer-to-peer collaboration, and gig ecosystems. In other words, while maintaining a recognizable difference between full-scale entrepreneurs (i.e., owners of uniquely configured structures of capital assets) and hired, non-owning subordinates, these developments nonetheless call for a substantial extension of the entrepreneurial (or at least quasi-entrepreneurial) function to agents traditionally regarded as passive and reactive in their professional orientation. This, as I have tried to emphasize repeatedly, is the essence of proactivity, the phenomenon whose widespread and unhampered practice offers a credible promise of expanding the creative role of every human being to the maximum extent compatible with the fact of individual variation in temperaments, talents, and inclinations.

Now, in line with the well-known biblical principle of "to whom much is given, much is required", it must be underscored once again that, given the multifaceted nature of proactivity, multiple interrelated challenges have to be met in order not to waste the potential inherent in it. As indicated earlier, these challenges range from resisting the siren song of economic nationalism and UBI-style welfarism to building robust local networks of high-quality social capital and learning to use deceptively effective informational tools in a cognitively mature fashion. As such, they demand sustained multidisciplinary cooperation on a global scale among all those individuals who are especially sensitive to the increasingly essential role of proactivity in a society that has already reaped the majority of the benefits afforded by the managerial model.

Thus, to invoke a term mentioned in the preceding chapter, the individuals in question can be regarded as paradigmatically meta-proactive: that is, devoted to the promotion of proactivity by means of safeguarding the institutional and civilizational preconditions for its flourishing. Needless to add, accomplishing this task successfully requires pooling together a number of theoretically and practically complementary perspectives, including that of a perceptive economic analyst who wields timeless logical tools in addressing timely anthropological developments, a shrewd entrepreneur who spearheads novel organizational techniques in dealing with unusual business contingencies, and a prudent customer who devises personalized filters of reliability in a world of marketing chaos.

While each of these perspectives generates numerous instances of individually beneficial proactivity, all of them may also produce positive externalities in the form of stimulating illustrations of the many ways in which the concept under consideration can open new avenues for value productivity. This, in turn, may steadily increase the analytical clarity with which economic agents approach the implementation of proactive measures, stripping it of buzzwordy vagueness, platitudinous obscurity, and feel-good irrelevance.

It is my hope that, as far as theoretical contributions to the study of proactivity are concerned, the present work has gone some way to advancing this clarity, thereby adding a meaningful building block both to economic science and to its timely practical applications. In other words, it is my hope that it added to the reader's understanding of human action as the mainspring of developmental creativity, personal dynamism, resilient adaptability, and other essential elements of both individual flourishing and its broader socioeconomic, vigorously cooperative ramifications.

Index

For Product Safety Concerns and Information please contact our
EU representative GPSR@taylorandfrancis.com Taylor & Francis
Verlag GmbH, Kaufingerstraße 24, 80331 München, Germany